THE UNIVERSAL
BIBLE

My Understanding, My Belief

RAKIM THE GODMAN

MILTON & HUGO L.L.C.
4407 Park Ave., Suite 5
Union City, NJ 07087, USA

Website: *www. miltonandhugo.com*
Hotline: *1- 888-778-0033*
Email: *info@miltonandhugo.com*

Ordering Information:
Quantity sales. Special discounts are granted to corporations, associations, and other organizations. For more information on these discounts, please reach out to the publisher using the contact information provided above.

Library of Congress Control Number: 2025901972
ISBN-13:   979-8-89285-431-3   [Paperback Edition]
                  979-8-89285-432-0   [Digital Edition]

Rev. date: 01/14/2025

Contents

The Book Of Religion

Religion: A body of beliefs and practices regarding the supernatural, and the practice of one or more deities

Chapter 1

(1:1) There are hundreds of different religions across the world. (1:2) They all, in turn, have their own code of conduct and Practices. Their creeds vary, Defending the things such as race birthplace, and ancestry, or quite simply the teaching oof those that raised them, which were passed down through generations of elders of home and community. (1:3) There are in fact so many different religions. That often caused me to question both which one should I let myself believe in, or should I believe in any of them at all.

(1:4) Each respective religion has their own understanding of how all creation came to be. (1:5) How the universe, and all that exist when we were created, as well as by whom they were created. (1:6) Is there one God responsible for all things seen and unseen? Or are there Multiple gods who a contribution to the overall perfection of existence?

(1:7) I will never truly know the answers to these questions. For to know I would have had to be present at the beginning of creation. (1:8) There are prominent religions that are practiced by millions. There are modest religions practiced by thousands. There is unrecognized religion in the world that are practiced by hundreds in small villages known and unknown in location and, and there are personal religions only practiced but the one who created it. (1:9) There are many religions that are not in agreeance with each other about anything, while there are also some with minimal details that differentiate them. (1:10) Regardless, no matter how much they may coincide or oppose each other. There is one thing that they all have in common, that they all are believers. (1:11) Believers that believe in and practice them may vary in comparison from a range of millions in one particular religion depending which one, to another where it may it be just the one believer who chooses to identify and articulate their own set of belief's they themselves recognize as their own religion.

(1:12) Many who practice the more popular religion's tend to shun, or in some cases even shame others that choose to believe in a religion that isn't the same as their own. (1:13) They make the mistake of thinking their own religion is somehow more plausible than another. (1:14) It's my understanding that plausibility is of the mind while faith is of the heart. (1:15) I don't approach religion based on what makes the most sense to me, I instead approach the feeling of the word of a particular religion puts into my heart. (1:16) While the brain is incapable of comprehending many things classified as supernatural, the heart has a mind of its own. (1:17) The mind has a voice, and that voice speaks through a feeling. (1:18) a feeling of intuition I must accept as my own truth, leaving others to do the same regarding themselves. (1:19) In the end no one that exists can prove that their religion is better or truer than another. (1:20) One religion having more believers than another doesn't equate to more truth in it. It only means there are more people who accept it as their own truth. (1:21) I understand that there is a difference.

Chapter 2

(2:1) Whether it is texts found on scrolls in caves and cavers that date back to ancient times, writing or records of proclaimed prophets and ancient teachers unearthed carvings and drawings discovered in ancient temples that date back thousands of years. I understand none of these by any means is irrefutable evidence that means which were recorded discovered or rediscovered are in fact true. (2:2) Instead they simply mean, that the people wrote those writings and, drew the drawing or built the temples held those particular set of beliefs. That, as spoken, does not mean they are true. Just to those people or artists. (2:3) What those perspective people chose to believe due to whatever life experiences or teachings they lived through or learned that caused them to accept those things as true to them. (2:4) In accepting those things as true to them when their hearts and minds is ultimately what helped manifest that source of power in which they drew their own strength from, through faith.

(2:5) I believe the simple fact at the center of the idea of religion to be that no matter how popular or implausible one may be. What ultimately makes the beliefs of a religion true is that it is accepted by the people who practice it as true to them. (2:6) the fact that they believe it makes it true to them and that's all that matters to them.

(2:7) I will never truly know if there is one God, or many Gods, If the creator is a man or woman, A thing or if there is even a God after all. (2:9) All I can do as a human being confined to small percentage of accessibility to consciousness is were way to the right side of the room, as the details flashed, he stopped the spankings, because to find something higher than oneself to believe in. (2:10) Believe in it for whatever reasons you choose to believe in it for and stand firm in that belief because it's all you will ever have in the matter. (2:11) That's the true beauty of religion and faith, not being able to "know" anything to be factual, but still believe none the less (2:12) No matter how much sense a scientist, or a prophet may make it does not their word true. (2:13) I understand that sometimes an outright lie can make perfect sense and the outright truth can sometimes make no sense at all. (2:14) Knowing this relying solely on reason. Ut's no way for me to live life. (2:15) When seeking to understand the Mysticism of humanities origin. The average human mind is incapable of reaching the level of consciousness it would take to get in tone with the creator. (2:16) I believe that if one does reach that level and experience some form of truth one to take as their own personally. (2:17) Something to give an individual a personalized understanding to get through their own personal struggle with their faith. (2.19) When one approaches the IDGA of religion they often compare the multitude of religions then choose what suits their understanding best. (2.19) Others follow numbers, figures that since one has more people who practice that that's the most logical route to take. (2:20) I believe that I can send one down a path that wasn't meant for them to walk, and they will have no true inner connection to that religion. (2:21) They'd be mere partitioners and not true believers!

Chapter 3

(3:1) One must follow the heart. Mot the brain. (3:2) The brain has limitation of comprehension so it cannot be trued. Trusted with matters such as this. (3:3) Nor should one attempt or push their own beliefs onto others, then they get angry when one pushes back because they choose not to accept it as their own. (3:4) Some take offense if someone opposes or refuse not to crossover and that by all means it selfish and wrong on many levels. (3:5) No man should ever trouble another for their religion. (3:6) One must accept and respect what others chose to embrace as their truth regardless if it is the exact opposite of their own. (3:7) I understand that it is necessary for multiple religions to exists. How deep would the understanding of religion truly be able to get if there were no opposition to raise certain questions. (3:8) If all humanity knew all there is to know then the world wouldn't be as it is today. (3:9) There would be no sense of diversity, and diversity is what make the world so beautiful. (3:10) It's what allows one to help another and give unique understanding that further on the mind of those who seek understanding. (3:11) Religion will be debated for eternity. (3:12) A Day when all humanity shares the same understanding is both unfathomable as well as unforeseeable, so to achieve that impossibility is not the goal of these words. (3:13) Instead this message is to bring together all the believers in a universal way. (3.14) Using beliefs as the glue to solidify a universal oneness to all respective understandings and beliefs of who or what God truly is. (3.15) Using belief as the glue to solidify a universal oneness to all respective understandings and beliefs of who or what God truly is. (3:16) To show that the universe itself, is responsible for all there is. (3.17) To archive that goal would be beauty in an unprecedented form.

(3.18) After all it's my understanding that all believers are praying to the same source of creation, they just call them different names. (3.19) They also use different means and rituals to communicate with those sources directly. (3.20) In the end, all paths of true believers undoubtedly lad to the same destination. (3.21) No matter the road traveled to make it to enlightenment all parts begin and end the same.

The Book of Truth

Truth: An Accepted statement. Proposition or theory: Honesty the real state of things: The body of real events facts: when one believes and accepts as facts

Chapter 1

(1:1) I believe one individual truth, is to divorce from the truth itself. (1:2) While truth itself reigns supremely divine and all knowing: My individual truth as a being is based solely on what I choose to believe or not to believe. (1:3) Since "Truth" itself is often inaccessible to humanity, especially to humans. All I can do to aid in finding the truth is to rely on one or two things. (1:4) The first is reason I believe the reason is the start of the brain. (1:5) Where one used their own intellect and common sense to figure out what's the most plausible truth or falsehood in any given scenario. (1:6) The second of the two is they may use their intuition. intuition is strictly of the heart. (1:7) Where one uses their own feeling and instinct to sense what they feel to be the truth or false hood in any given scenario.

(1:8) My brain processes the facts of a given situation and determines what will or should be processed as truth based on plausibility. In Lamen terms. What make the most sense. (1:9) Being exclusively on plausibility can often lead to me accepting false hood as my truth. (1:10) I always remind myself that "Truth" sometimes makes no plausible sense at all, while an outright lie can sometimes make all the logical sense in the world, yet still be a world away from "Truth" itself. (1:11) In these instances, I turn to my intuition, knowing my heart, simultaneously processes these same given facts and determines what to ultimately accept as truth based of the feelings that those facts given produce within my intuition. (1:12) That "gut feeling" in the pit of my stomach that never lies. (1:13) However, While the intuition never lies. I must still be careful not confine myself that I feel something that I actually don't feel. (1:14) Relying solely on intuition may be too advance for the average person. (1:15) I understand I'm not always able to fully separate myself from my brain in order to truly tune into the intuition of my heart, and that's what ultimately can lead to me accepting falsehood as my truth. (1:16) As well I must stay aware that the feelings are wrong to the core can be falsely vindicated by my brain in order to make me believe that it doesn't feel wrong for the reasons it feels wrong which then leads to me ignoring the voice of intuition that I always hear through feeling. (1:17) One may ask, if they cannot solely rely on the brain, nor can they rely solely on the heart then where does that truly leave them? (1:18) My understanding to that question is that it leaves oneself at the very center of the war between two entities caught in the cross fire between thoughts and feelings. (1:19) Left to fend for themselves, fend for themselves, understand for themselves and then choose for themselves exactly who they want to be, via action.

(1:20) I believe the brain attempts to convince the heart to accept something as truth, when it knows that something is false, just as a test of self, therefore attempting to override feelings by way of mental justification. (1:21) Hence, I believe that the popular saying, "Never let your emotion override your intellect," coincides with that theory.

Chapter 2

(2:1) Even though the saying can be accurate, I understand that its only to the extent of the level of consciousness possessed by someone who is in tune with their feelings. (2:2) A feeling can be a lie detector, but only to one who possess the ability to separate the two powers at war within. (2:3) The war ensues within all. On a daily basis down to a per toughly basis, never ending and infinite. thought vs feeling. (2:4) I believe this war for the acceptance of the truth or false hood is the push and the pull that leads to the making of one's self. (2:5) The self represents the decision that is made and is then empowered by the victor of each battle fought. (2:6) The self sits at the center what is being asked to pick a side to accept as their truth. For instance, the making of self is what solidifies what I accept as my truth. (2:7) My truth is what ultimately shapes my perspective and worldly views. These self-accepted views, in turn create my own personal universe where what I believe "IS."

(2:8) A tale of a war for truth and how they affect people differently in everyday life based on perspective. Two toddlers play in the living room, while their mother prepare dinner in the kitchen, and their father prepares the dinner table in the dining room. They live in a rebuilt home that was burnt down with two children inside that passed. As their mother cook, she yells for the children to stop playing in the living room before something gets broken. The toddlers immediately stop playing and their mother and father can hear that they did even though they couldn't physically see them. One minute later a lamp suddenly falling from the living room shelf and shattering on the floor. The two toddlers were 100percent not the cause of the lamp falling from the shelf and they know the exact cause because they themselves witnessed what happened. Both the mother and the father run into the living room to find the lamp shattered on the floor to the left of the room while both toddlers sat to the right with fear in their eyes when they looked at their parents. The mother says didn't I tell y'all to stop playing before y'all break something, she then turned to the father and ordered him to spank them both since they didn't want to listen. The toddlers began to cry stating that it wasn't them who broke the lamp it was the two other kids that knocked it from the shelf. Their father scolding look fades.

(2:9) Those are the facts of the situation, now comes the war of the brain vs the heart, intellect vs. intuition. Within both the mother and father separately.

(2:10) The mother uses her brain to solve the dilemma. The kids were still playing after she told them to stop. That lead to the lamp being broken and now the look of fear in the toddler's eyes is for anticipation of punishment so they together are trying to say they are not the blame, which make no logical sense. (2:11) This application of reason is more plausible than believing that two unseen children conveniently broke the lamp at that particular time. She decides to believe that her children are responsible, so her order for them to be spanked is justified in her mind, she ignores the feeling in her heart that wants to believe her children. (2:12) The father on the other hand uses his heart to solve the dilemma. He could feel in his intuition that his children were telling the truth. That they were in fact not responsible for breaking the lamp.

(2:13) Immediately his brain gives reason to ignore his intuition and focus on the logic. Eventually logic wins and he decides to ignore what he felt deep down and proceeds to spank the children per order of his wife.

(2:14) As he spanks the toddlers a sense of guilt overcame him internally and flashes of details of incident began to pass through his mind that he ignored before making the decision to side with his side. (2:15) First, he clearly heard the children stop playing when their mother told them to. the lamp didn't fall until at least a minute late, and even then, the kids he was no longer sure what to accept as the truth at that point. The war between the brain and the heart was to back and forth for him. (2:16) While neither parent could ever in fact know the truth of the situation was from their perspective places. The toddlers on the other end witnessed something that they were certain wasn't something their parents would ever believe. The children's truth however was all that mattered to them in the end because they know what they witnessed. (2:17) whether their parents believed them or not. This the war that takes place within all on a daily basis. In their perspective lives there in search of the truth of their own situations, circumstances, and dynamics may vary as well as the roles of those involved, however the war for truth itself is ever occurring and everlasting. (2:18) Ultimately, the winner of the war gets to claim victory of the self. (2:19) There will be another war to follow soon after, therefore there will be no time to celebrate the victory. The next war will again send the self-back to its position the center waiting to be claimed yet again. (2:20) Once each was is lost or won, the self is established, truth is accepted and it is then on to the next. I believe these wins and losses are what ultimately makes up how people view life as an individual. How their life perspectives are a result of the wins and losses of those internal battles for their own truths. One's truth is what make them who they are. (2:21) However, one must always remember that their truth is not always the same as Truth itself. I believe long as one accepts their own truth then that's all that should ever matter because that's the closest, they'll ever be able to get to Divine truth itself.

The Book Of Purpose

Purpose: An Objective or result aimed at; intention: Reason of being.

Chapter 1

(1:1) While purpose is given to all at birth, its sadly seldom found, due to selfishness of one personal want needs. (1:2) Most spend their entire lives searching for purpose. They seek to understand why their power put them here. (1:3) They search to find what it is that make them happy what is it that makes them feel whole. Most of all, what make them rich! (1:4) As individuals, we all start our journey on different paths. The journey however, begins at the same time, and that at our own birth. (1:5) Unbeknownst to many, we have been sent to the world with a specific mission to carry out to the best of our ability. What we must accept is that although our individual paths will vary from person to person, all of our purpose boil down to the same objective goal. That's to be .... (1:6) As youths we naturally take to activities and hobbies such as sports, entertainment, writing painting etc. through these things we find natural talents in which were either blessed with at birth or they develop a deep connection to then put into practice to become the best we could possibly become because we weren't a natural at it to start.

(1:7) One child is born a natural at playing sports, another child develops a connection to that same sport, however isn't good at to begin with like the child who is a natural. One teen finds they had the natural ability to sing graciously all along. Another teen suddenly develops a connection to singing however, their voice is not as good to start one adult realizes they are a natural at authoring. Another adult develops a connection to writing but their way of painting with articulation isn't as good as the natural. So on and so forth. As time goes on and the one who has the connection, minus the natural talent, put in the time, energy, effort to study and practice to become the best they can possibly be, they'll realize that they could ultimately reach the same level no matter what the task may be. No matter the goal. No matter the objective. Determination breeds success, and success at a craft can ultimately led to being financially successful in life, which is usually the all-end goal for most people. (1:8) Once they have achieved financial success at whatever path they chose they usually convince themselves that they are fulfilled. (1:9) Does this mean that this person has found his or her purpose? Because they found success in what they do mean that. That's their purpose in life? If we can do anything we set our minds to by putting in the time, energy, and effort then how could the craft mattered be purpose itself? (1:10) Does the fact that one is good at something mean that's their purpose in life? That is their reason for existing? I believe that the answers to these questions to be no!

(1:11) To me, we all have a unique purpose in life and it's all individual based. While the paths we choose to take in life can lead to us to success in many different ways, and on many different scales, our true purpose in life is what we do for those that need us after we've found success! (1:12) I believe that all our purposes in life are first to learn to grow, excel at whatever path we choose to take and simply us the success that the path has borne us and be all we can be. Not just for ourselves but for all the people in our lives that will need us, As well as the people who are not in our lives physically but will still need the benefits from our efforts and life's work from afar. (1:13) We to must realize that success doesn't apply exclusively to financial means. (1:14) Success can also be found in knowledge and wisdom, purpose is also being served, just on an internal scale which should be viewed as no less important than the physical means. (1:5) Each one teaches one, to put the student in position to be the teacher. When the teacher is made, the cycle should continue to infinity. (1:16) That too is undoubtedly one serving purpose through internal success. Which is just as needed, and should be just as appreciated!

(1:17) Physically giving back to those in need through Non-Profit organizations, charities and giveaways are a large-scale way of serving purpose through giving back. However, that should never discourage those on a smaller scale who may not have the mean to establish such organizations. (1:18) It also should never discourage those who don't have anything physical to give back because internal means are Just as important. (1:19) Our purpose is to simply uplift. To uplift in any form or fashion one can think of! (1:20) No Idea can be too small on the scale because every gram counts. As long as we are able, we should do. (1:21) The passing down of knowledge and wisdom is just as important to those in need as any other form of giving back in some cases maybe even more important. Saying the right thing at the right time to the right person in need sometimes do more, do more to impact a person's life than writing a check can!

Chapter 2

(2:1) How much would the check do, without the knowledge on what should be done with it? The check could be gone by the days end. (2:2) The knowledge however could last a person's life time if spoken at the right time, on the right manner! (2:3) A homeless woman doesn't have food to help feed a newly homeless man she meets. However, she knows of a place that often helps people in their unfortunate situations so she takes him there with her and the two eat together. (2:4) Is that not her serving purpose through knowledge? Is that her giving back none the less to a person who has nothing, a simple meal is everything! (2:5) A person with nothing themselves to physically offer, passing down he knowledge of something someone or someplace else has to offer, can be the determining factor of another living or dying, we just must always remember that every gran on the scale counts towards the cause! (2:6) Giving back is our true purpose, the way we choose to or are able to should never be seen as to small. I am aware that God is always watching always listening, and most importantly always testing us. (2:7) Blessings will always be given naturally when you don't chase them!

The Book Of Change

Change: To make or become different: To Alter: To replace with another.

Chapter 1

(1:1) Change is ever constant, never ending, unescapable, yet in some cases often registered. (1:2) Sometimes change is registered intentionally, and other times more often seen change is registered subconsciously. (1:3) As time passes, we will all change. We all Evolve. We start as children who look to our mothers and fathers for all the answers to solve all the problems, to bridge all the gaps and as we learn from watching them handle things for us, we then evolve into beings who can do the for ourselves. Some of us learn by watching and naturally do them for ourselves when the opportunity arrives others are taught. (1:4) Change can be seen in two different ways. Change can also be felt to one who is in tune with the energy produced by people places and things in the universe. (1:5) the obvious way change can be seen is through physical growth or physical reconstruction. A child grows into a teen, A teen grows into an adult an adult grows into an elder. (1:6) Their physical features mature as their age does but if one puts in the time energy and effort, they can preserve their body's health and functionality to increase their lifespan. They can exercise regularly, eat health, and stay active and as they mature in age physically, they will usually feel younger than they actually are. This change is evident because its physically seen.

(1:7) The more important form of change happens eternally. As people change physically there is also a change that takes place inside of them. They way they think, the way they feel, their views, their principles, their morality and their values. (1:8) These are the things that actually make a person. These are the things that a person individualism and shows those who encounter who they are dealing with. (1:9) Things like hate, resentment, anger, fear, etc. Are usually taught or subconsciously imbedded into people at a young age by the people in their lives or around them in a close enough proximity to influence them long term. (1:10) A racist person teaches their children to hate another person because the color of their skin. They teach their children that they are better or superior for whatever reasons they. They feel they are or for whatever reasons they were themselves were taught They are which came from whomever taught them.

(1:11) As time passes, the child who was taught to hold these ill-advised beliefs will grow and project these views onto others that they come across in life. Eventually they will cross paths with someone who oppose those beliefs and inform them that that are the beliefs of a racist. (1:12) That ill-advised person will do one of two things over time. They will stand firm in their beliefs and not allow the opposing party to cloud their judgement or they will feel something inside them change as the opposition advocates which will cause them to see things a bit differently. (1:13) Upon accepting hat they were taught to have views which didn't truly reflect their nature as an individual. They will go through a change and from that point forward they'll lead their lives with a new found understanding. (1:14) They'll trat people know as an equal as opposed to less than. They'll express more compassion for those that look different than them. They'll become better people individually! (1:15) The change isn't exclusive to the fomentation. It can be applied to many different situations and scenarios, where a person just experiences a change of heart. (1:16) Following the change usually comes resentment or anger towards those who taught that person their old beliefs or sometimes it could lead to a feeling of sorrow for those hold that old belief because they know the feeling living in anger can produce.

(1:17) Some will feel abandoned because they themselves didn't go through the change themselves, therefore causing the inability to fathom the change itself. If they don't agree they began to view you now as the opposition, and if you can't get them to understand that is usually were friendships or relationships end and people grow apart. Its either that or they learn together, grow together and strengthen their bonds, which is seldom seen, or there is usually only one black sheep in here. (1:18) The change takes place in all of us at different times and when it does take place it paramount that we acknowledge the change after that we must make the physical changes need to be more in order to accommodate the internal change. (1:19) this will call for sacrifices, whether they be removing people, from your life letting go of material attachment's, putting distance between places you us to frequent. These sacrifices are usually the hardest part of the change to accept because the sacrifices will be the people places and things you love the most. They will be the things we may feel we can't live without. The sacrifices are the part of the change which can cause one to resist changing. (1:20) It becomes hard for us to see ourselves apart from those people we love, but we must realize that just because we have love for a person doesn't mean they are supposed to be in our lives.

We have to learn to love from a distance. (1:21) Those are the people who bring more negative into our lives that positive. More destruction that fulfillment, both internally and physically, we must set aside the love we have for them and go off their actions. The sacrificing of material things symbolizes the internal detachment of possessions in the physical word.

Chapter 2

(2:1) In a material world where most people base success on how much material possessions one has, material wealth is more sought after that internal wealth. (2:2) People spend more effort towards projecting an image of wealth through material than actually being financially stable. They live beyond their means to keep up an appearance, when one can find it in them to separate themselves from material shackles, they can finally experience another level of internal freedom and a deeper view of what wealth truly is. That's the change. (2:3) What's a car to piece of land?

(2:4) After the change take place and he people and places and things that us to mean the most to us are suddenly the farthest from our mind we must use the new found time and energy to learn to put the needs of others before your own. (2:5) To not be driven by your wants and accept that all that will be needed will be provided at all times. You will be given continuous, compassion, and Faith above all. (2:6) The important thing when we go through the change is to help change as many as we can on our way. The more people who experience the change as individuals, the sooner we can began to change the world itself.

The Book Of Dreamers

Dreamer: One deeply in tune with the thoughts, images and emotions that occur during a state of sleep.

Chapter 3

(3:3) Get in tone with your emotions learn to lead those that need guidance and protect those who need to be protected. As soon as we learn to do these things in the safe confines of dream world, we can then see how we will naturally apply those things into the way we live our lives in the physical world. (3:4) A mature dreamer will still have moments where they might fall short, but they will never lose sight of the goal which is master of all fear and negative emotions. This mastery enables me with love, peace and patience of the eternal world. (3:5) After sometime years, or even decades of being a mature dreamer, the mature dreamer comes to a place where the instinctively flow through he dreamworld doing all that is right even when sometimes it may feel wrong, that's when they reach the stage of the wise dreamer. One who has survived the test of times and live a selfless life both in the physical and the internal world. (3:6) The wise dreamer will usually be older in age, however if a younger person in age put in the energy and effort to achieving mature then wise dreamer capabilities, it is fully possible for them to earn it. To earn it is all up to the seeker. And it is all preparation for what is to come upon the arrival of death. The life after. Dreams are one of my biggest intrigues when it comes to cap abilities of the human mind. I often seek resolve to problems I face.

Chapter 1

(1:2) I often see the future, present and the past, through premonitions and Daja Vue all in the dream world. (1:3) Hidden sometimes in plain sight, and other times deeply in the chaos of the dream often lies secrete knowledge of things to come in my life. Other times to clarify and understanding of things that have already passed. (1:4) Whatever the case, the only way to make sense of the meaning behind the events of the dream is to actually put the energy into seeking understanding. (1:5) If you don't devote time and energy into seeking, the enlightenment will never be given, for enlightenment is earned. That while everyone may in fact have dreams, not everyone dreams as often as or the same as what I consider to be a dreamer. Tome there is a noticeable distinction between a person who dreams and a dreamer. (1:7) true by nature at some point during sleep we all dream weather we remember upon awakening or not. (1:8) A person who dreams has a hard time recollecting the dream itself. They forget a majority but remember a part or two. Sometimes more than none they remember most parts but forget the most important parts which are usually small. The recollection vanishes instantly upon awakening. (1:9) That's one of the things that separates a person who dreams from a dreamer. They go through the dream as a passenger while the dreamer navigates as a driver. (1:10) The dreamer seeks enlightenment in the dream world all before entering while inside and upon awaking. They set their intention to searching for clues, answers and understanding and often keep records of patterns, events times numbers, words spoken settings, and appearances of people. (1:11) The random things stand out in a dream to a dreamer because they are aware that random in a dream can equate to vital in the physical world. (1:12) A person who dreams, do just that and only that and that only, "have dreams". Upon waking. They often dismiss them chalking them off as pure imagination, with no relevance to the physical world. They give the dream itself no thought. They see it as unreal and unnecessary to seek understanding they simply don't care to care, the Polar opposite of a dreamer. (1:13) the most important thing that a person who dreams goes through the experience of the dream with no true power to change outcome of what can or will occur. They simply accept the events that ensure in the dream whether they like them or not, then awake from it full of whatever emotions the dream itself brought them to feel. The dreamer however only starts at that stage, they aren't content with not being able to react according to the moral standards. They themselves hold in the physical world. (1:14) they devote the time, thought and energy into seeking enlightenment of the dream worlds. As time passes and they show the dream maker God. Seeking that gift of enlightenment, they start to be given moments where the door of consciousness is opened for them. (1:15) In the dream suddenly all of their senses are heightened to the level of supernatural, and they find themselves 100% conscience that they are awake inside the dream world. (1:16) Their adrenaline kick into overdrive and excitement of free range of thought gives way to selfishness wants and desires. They are aware that they can suddenly think, say, or do whatever they want and get away with it because they see it as just the dream world. They are aware they now have the power to manifest into the dream. Anything the desire all they have to do is set their thoughts to it and will it into existence in an instant. (1:17) they can make things appear just by thinking or saying to themselves "I want this" or "I need that" and in a blink of an eye, there it will be! (1:18) This is the gift. This is the blessing to those who refer to the dreamworld as more than just some place in our imagination that plays tricks on us causing us to think something s real only to take it all away from us upon awakening. (1:19) A dreamer fact a real place, it's just in a different reality on the other side of the physical world! (1:20) While the gift of conciseness is no small thing to the dream world one must beware that the goal is mastery of consciousness in the dream. (1:21) It may take time for a young dreamer to ever realize that the door of conscience has been open briefly for them in the past. This is because it all can happen so fast, and at times may only last for a few seconds.

Chapter 2

(2:1) Consciousness it may be a brief as you being afraid of something or someone in a dream and you tell yourself you want to wake up, so you will in all reality that could have been yourself to awaken yourself. An opportunity to overcome something that brings you fear of harm or death in the physical world. In that sense you fail the test. Because you chose to flee. (2:2) Maybe an animal is chasing you, or a person with a weapon and the fear of what may happen if they get to you cause you to wake yourself. Whatever the case, you must understand that the door of consciousness was opened to you, and you chose to close it out of fear. (2:3) With your power to choose you could easily choose to stand in courage and confidence that couldn't harm you even if they tried. (2:4) You could've willed yourself some form of protection and saw it through. You had the power to do anything in the world, instead you chose to close the door out of fear and leave the dream. Fear is a natural reaction to a young dreamer but as they mature and become more enlightened, they learn to address the natural reactions so they can make the right decisions no matter what fear the dream brings them to face. It's all just a test, fear is just an obstacle. (2:6) Another thing a young dreamer often does when the doorway to consciousness is open and they find themselves free to think freely is they usually do is something is wrong or something selfish. (2:7) They seldom look to see what the dream is asking them. The only way to know what the dream is calling for is to analyze the setting and try to get an understanding of what's going on. When you know what's going on you can make just decisions on what exactly on what it is that you are supposed to be doing. Think of what the dream maker may want not what you want.

(2:8) A male young dreamer may see a female in his dream when the doors to consciousness opens and upon realizing he is in control of himself, he off of pure male instinct first thing that may come to his mind. 99% of the time that will be sexual. Hell decides that he wants to have sex with that woman and with no rearguard for what the woman may want the will proceed even if it means against he will. (2:9) The fact that he will see it as just a dream he will use that as an excuse to not bother to ask her consent. He will chase the nirvanic feeling of sex and orgasms in the dream which can ultimately bare physical fruit in the form of him ejaculating in his sleep. This is what to be considered a wet dream. (2:10) In dreams we can feel physical sensations, and real raw emotions. If sex in a dream can cause one to ejaculate on physical world or cry real teas in the physical then how can we believe that the dream doesn't hold any sense of realness? (2:11) How can it all be pure imagination when the emotions and sensations themselves are real? A dreamer is aware that just because it takes place all in your mind doesn't mean that it's not real, its real to you if you feel it and that's all those mattes. (2:12) As young dreamer progresses over time, they will become aware of something that will cause them to reevaluate their own decisions making in the dreamworld when the door to consciousness is open. (2:13) Once they realize the consequence of the selfishness of their wants, they will long to make better decisions so they can be rewarded with more time in the dream. More time to feel the surreal feelings and emotions of the dream world that can only be appreciated by another dreamer. One who understands the experience on a personal level. (2:14) the feeling of peace and freedom. The feeling of heaven. (2:15) One must realize that consciousness in the dream world is an honored gift of power. (2:16) That power is not given for you to go and do what you please. It is given to you so that you may have the strength and ability to do whatever it is that the dream may call for you to do. (2:17) One must realize that with great power comes great responsibility, and in the dream, world is where we practice through trial and error, doing the right thing! Regardless what the situation or the circumstances may be, we must learn to use that power to put others needs before their own. This is what grants us more time in the dream. (2:18) We must learn to analyze the setting and events of the dream to determine what action the dream may be calling for them to take, then we must make them. (2:19) How much fear they may feel, or any other emotion that maybe blocking them from carrying out their mission. Should be ignored because they just obstacles (2:20) when we are finally able to start making the unselfish decisions, we will then prove to the dream maker that we are trying our best to hold ourselves, to the same moral standards in the dream world as we hold ourselves in the physical world. (2:21) They then, and then only, will graduate to the level and title of a mature dreamer.

Chapter 3

(3:1) A mature dreamer is aware that the dream world is a safe space for them to overcome their fears they may have in the physical world. (3.2) When they can address flaws, where they can peacefully overcome things like lust, hate, and selfishness. Where they can.

The Book Of Life & Death

Life: The quality that distinguishes a vital and functional being from a dead body or inanimate matter: The physical and mental experiences of an individual.

Chapter 1

(1:1) Many people were taught to only acknowledge life itself in its physical form. (1:2) Because we knowledge life the movement of people, place, things. I believe it cause us to believe that that perception is everything. (1:4) How we chose to see life is what separates us as individual's beings as a whole. Perception breeds the individualism of a soul. (1:5) Hence, while many see life as physical as a universal life strictly in its essential from which is eternal. What goes on, on the inside of life itself can only be seen through the action of movement. (1:6) However, I believe true life is the unseen force that powers the people places and things, not the people places and thing themselves. (1:7) For the are just vessels for which life serves it purpose through. (1:8) life in that essence is the interna force that enables the external matter to perform in a physical manor, and serve whatever purpose it was created to serve. (1:9) As complex as science would portray life to be I myself believe life in existence come down to three core components. These three components together are what I understand and accept to be "my universe" trinity. (1:10) What we think, what we feel and lastly what we do. Thought, feeling and action! The entire human experience boils down to this "universal Trinity". It's just that simple.

(1:11) Thought, I believe, is the first of the universal trinity, which to me represents consciousness. The awareness that you exist as an individual, free to think your own thoughts and make your own commands to the body through thought (1:12) I understand and believe consciences and awareness can be individual's". I believe the soul resides in the domain of the brain. (1:13) All individual souls come from the same source which is "the Soul "itself. (1:14) We are all given "A soul upon conception which is in fact a micro cast off from a macro. (1:15) A chip off the block so to speak. I believe this to be the mother (1:16) She is to be all thought, all conscience all knowing. She is the source of all knowledge and wisdom. I believe her to be symbolically our mother. The mother soul, in which all individual souls come from, just as a mother land, or mother ship or mother board, which reflect her nature. (1:17) Feelings I believe this is the supernatural side of everyone's being that too, is all knowing, The source of all courage and strength all anticipating, and unfoolable. (1:18) It gives the ability to an individual to feel for themselves, and also give commands to the body through subconscious intuition. (1:19) This to be an "spirit" all individual spirits come from the same source, which is the spirit, itself. (1:20) In addition to a soul upon conception, I believe we all are given a spirit of our own, which too is just the of the macro individualized "chip off the old block" so to speak. (1:21) As I accept soul as the mother, I accept spirit as the father. His nature polar opposite of hers. I believe he resides in the domain of the heart completely separate from thought.

Chapter 2

(2:1) The soul and the spirit are trapped in an infinite internal war with one another. Such is their nature, their purpose within every living being. The internal war is endless, from birth to the return (2:2) 365 Days a year, 30 days a month, 7 days a week, 24 hours a day, all the way down to every thought of every second (2:3) I believe the purpose the purpose of the war between the soul and the spirit within us all is for the purpose of aiding and us in finding internal balance. (2:4) However, if balance isn't found and maintained the winner of, he battles gets control of the third component of the universal trinity, the body!

(2:5) The body itself represents action! (2:6) The body is most important to the experience of living life as a human (2:7) It's the temple which houses the soul and the spirit. (2:8) Still, at the same time the body is least important because it's the only one of the universal trinity's which is expendable. (2:9) Since the body represents action, it represents what we chose to do. The actions we choose to take given the thoughts temptations of the mind(soul) and the assurances/warnings of the heart (spirit) (2:10) One may argue that there are more than three components that are essential to life, and this must be addressed to explain the distinction. This argument would refer to the 5 senses. Sight, Touch, Taste, Smell, hearing. (2:11) I believe the distinction between the 5 senses and the universal trinity is that one applies to life as a whole and the other or only applies to the life of, the particular human body itself. (2:12) the 5 senses don't determine life or death as a whole because life itself will still go on in a body absent one, multiple, or all of the 5 senses. Instead, they only relate exclusively to the human body and its function ability/ capabilities. Simply put the body isn't life itself, the bodies many capabilities can't determine life or death of the whole body as a whole. (2:13) Life goes on with the loss of sight. Life goes on without the sense of smell, life goes on with the loss of taste. Life goes on with the loss of sound and life goes on with the loss of feeling. (2:14) So no there are no comparison to thru universal trinity, but yes, they do however play a role in the quality of life one gets to experience as a human being, that much can be agreed. DEATH: The end of life: The cause of loss of life: The cause of ruin.

(2:15) All things must have polar opposite according to natures law. Death is that only of life, only there's a common grievance about what exactly death is What it entails. (2:16) As a universe I have my own understanding and belief of truth toward what it means to experience Death. This is because I've personally experienced it! (2:17) While life is the unseen force that powers matter internally, I believe death applies only to the seen, the physical. (2:18) Death is the separation of the internal life force from the external matter. (2:19) Death is specific to the physical. As universal, I only see death as the return to the unseen side of the universe. (2:20) While most were taught to believe that death ends the life of a person, as a universal I was shown that death only ends the life of a body a person temporally dwelled in not the person's life as a whole. (2:21) Instead, Death starts the process of the Return".

Chapter 3

(3:1) As previously spoken, I believe that conception, we were given a mind of our own also an instinct of our own, A gift from the universe. (3:2) Together the duo resides in the fetus as it grows and then comes forth into the world to then via birth to live, and grow, and mature on its life journey. (3:3) It's the same as physically getting an even number of chromosomes from your mother and Father, just on a unseen level. (3:4) At death, when the body dies and there is no longer a body to house the individual mind and instinct, then they "return" to that which they were cast from upon conception, they go home! (3:5) All of the individuals thoughts returns home so they can finally rest from internal chaos of thought. All of the individuals feeling return so they can rest from the conflicted feelings of intuition which is triggered by thought". They can finally dwell in infinite peace. (3:6) the return "Death" I was shown it means to rest from thought in the oneness of overall peace. (3:7) the return home, which is the unseen sense of the universe itself. (3:8) Simply put I believe to be given life is to cast out from home to experience existence as a human being. To think and feel for ourselves then when the inevitable of death comes for us and we then go back to the home we were cast away from. (3:9) From the universe we come, so to the universe we return.

Book Of The Afterlife

Afterlife: A continued existence after experiencing death physically

Chapter 1

(1:1) Many different religions or spiritual people believe that life doesn't in fact end after one die's (1:2) They believe that one's consciousness still goes on in a different reality, separate from the physical world they left behind. (1:3) Some reason performs rituals upon burial of the body that are believed to preserve the body itself so that the person who passed away may still inhabit that body when they arrive on the other side of physical life, they are buried with things that their loved ones believe they will need like treasures of gold and other riches to assure that they are success continues over on the other side. They truly believe that Death is not the end. (1:4) This new world, this new reality spoken of that the conscience is said to live on in is what I believe to be "the dream world" itself.

(1:5) Everyone wonders of and have their own theory of what he after life or what heaven is. We often try to imagine what it's like and we try to create the most perfect image in our minds in order to cancel any fears we may have of dying thus giving ourselves something to look forward to or anticipate after crossing over. (1:6) I believe the dream world is in fact the afterlife where one's soul can live on forever. With no fear of death because nothing can hurt them. There is no fear, no sickness, no death. (1:7) However just because one is in the afterlife doesn't mean they won't still have duties to fill. The universe will call on them to do the things and there will be no consequences if these things are not done. (1:8)

If and by the time one reaches the afterlife they will act on pure intuition, because at that point they will be connected to the dream world on a deeper level and will still be used more as a vessel that just being free to do whatever they want.

(1:9) I believe that in the afterlife you will act naturally as a wise dreamer. Never questioning yourself of what the afterlife will call on you to do. (1:10) You will act without having to be told. You will act according to the needs of the afterlife, not the wants of your individual self. (1:11) You will see, you will feel, you will think, you will smell, you will hear, All the senses will be at a supernatural level. You will have the ability to part seas if you are called on to lead people across waters, you will move mountains, for the safe passage of the people. You will protect and serve in any way that may be necessary for you to do and this will forever be your life for eternity. (1:12) You will do this happily and will be fulfilled for your reward will be to bear witness and to feel the supernatural feelings of the power of controlling the elements themselves. (1:13) You must also know that the feeling of gpd while this will be your true reality, it will be a true dream to those who are in attendance. You must know that if you see a loved one or even a stranger, you must know them in some form from some lifetime because they made it to your dream.

(1:14) If you have passed on from life and left loved ones behind, you may very well and very often be called on by those that still live on the other side. And you can use those opportunities when they see you in their dream to deliver messages in whichever way it's called on you to do. (1:15) Sometimes the message may be verbal and direct while other times the message will be indirect and meant for them to figure out on their own as a dreamer (1:16) You will know as the one in the afterlife that you must resist the urge to do or say mare than what is meant, depending on the setting and circumstances given allowed to you at the encounter. You will feel their pain, sadness happiness, or guilt or anger and in turn will want to ease it in any way that you can, which will at times be permitted, but you will accept when it's meant for them to make sense of it all themselves. This is to help them with their own grieving process on the other side of life. (1:17) Your natural instinct when you see them might be to say. "I'm ok". I'm still alive and life on this side is better than anyone could ever believe. But in all actuality might be called to say not one word at all and maybe called just to touch them on the shoulder. (1:18) That will be all that they would need from you to get your entire message across, and that will be enough for them at the visit. (1:19) You may visit once, or you may visit often, but every visit you will only do or say what is allowed and you will accept that wholeheartedly because you will understand that that's all that will be needed. And will never attempt to question you and why that's all that's needed. Even though they will question why that's all that was allowed on theirs. (1:20) The after life and the dream world are indeed the same place, the difference between the two is that one has yet to crossover to that permanent state of reality, they only visit temporarily. (1:21) One may remain in afterlife for an eternity, or one may be eventually reincarnated all together that decision is not up to us. We ultimately may continue to be reincarnated for as long as seen fit.

The Book Of War

World view War: A state of open and declared armed fighting between people, state, or nations: A state of conflict, hospitality, or antagonism. A struggle between two opposing forces for a particular end.

Chapter 1

(1:1) I believe war is often viewed from its final stage, which is where you have one person or a group on one side with their beliefs of wright, wrong or entitlement and another person or group on the other side with opposing beliefs of wright wrong or entitlement and the two are fighting for control of whatever may be at stake. (1:2) May it be just for the sake to live or it be for the territory of land and all its resources, this is what we are taught to believe the essence of war is. (1:3) In fact I believe that instead of the first, it is the last phase of war. (1:4) I understand and acknowledge only one war. That is the war that we all fight regardless of our color, culture, or demographic. The war that leads to the war that we eventually see between people, nations, countries. The war that takes place within us all. (1:5) The internal war, You vs. You!

(1:6) I believe that before a war ca take place on a physical level it must first take place inside one's self. (1:7) If the right version of you wins the war within, then there could be a possibility of no physical was taking place at all! A flawless victory! (1:8) A universal I believe that there are two versions of ourselves that dwell within us. We have the version of ourselves that we are born with our essence. Then we have the version of ourselves that life creates us to be, which ultimately becomes our ego. (1:9) When we are born, we are given a name by our parents, that birth name is the essence of our being. The pureness of us. (1:10) As we grow into our own beings and our life experiences mold us into whatever they mold us into, we in turn, create an alternate version of ourselves in which often times name something else. This is for instance a nick name or as a second name. (1:11) I believe that both your nick name and your birthname are not just name themselves, but they both are people. In nature. They are mentality. (1:12) Thes two versions of yourself are the two mentalities that go with war with one another to see who gets to control the actions of the body you reside in. (1:13) the version of ourselves that we were born is usually kind in its nature. Giving loving patient and all things associated with innocence. While on the other hand the version of ourselves that life creates us to be is usually the compete opposite of who we were born and I associate that side with trauma. (1:14) The two may have the same similarities but for the most part they are polar opposite. The quality is necessary for the for the war that is to take place for control of the body. (1:15) The way hey war with each other is internally, through thought and feeling. (1:16) One feels and thinks one way always wanting to react this way while the other feels and thinks the other way and wants to react the same way. (1:17) You "yourself sit in between the two and you are represented by the choice you decide to make. So, while you have two versions of you the side born and the side created, then comes, then comes the 3rd which is determined by the making of your mind and taking of your action. The thoughts themselves don't reflect your character only your essence of your trauma. It is the action themselves that determine who you chose to be! (1:18) I believe, no such thing as being all positive and condemning all negative, I believe it's about balancing the two and knowing which version of yourself you should let control at which time and for how long you should be that version before you let the other one take over.

It's about knowing which version of yourself to let drive and which version to let be the passenger. The universe will call for the act of balance and etiquette in turn make you the car, the passenger (which is usually the trauma side to take the reins in a scenario it's up to you as the vehicle to find out for how long to let that side be in control, because they may only have to serve a short purpose. (1:19) The version of ourselves we were born can be born a leader, but is often times born a naïve follower, susceptible to manipulated due to the over kindness. However the verses of ourselves created by trauma was molded by the darker side of life the side of as that's seen people take advantage of kindness. That side of us is know as the warrior. (1:20) This side usually protects the innocent side of us. (1:21) There is a chief and a warrior within us all and there will be times in life where the warrior will have to step in to serve his purpose no matter how righteous we live our lives.

Chapter 2

(2:1) Even though it's the negative experiences in life that mold the dark side of our being, I believe that doesn't mean that the dark side of our being is actually bad or negative as a whole. (2:2) Although our trauma side was born through negativity, it can still be used to serve in a positive way. (2:3) One may have to defend themselves, their loved ones, or even a stranger who is unable to protect themselves, and would call on the warrior within them to see themselves or other through. (2:4) One must understand that each side serves a purpose and in knowing that they must also understand that the negative is in fact necessary. (2:5) Negative don't always equate to bad (2:6) The Internal war can only take place with opposing views. Each view is a representation of the temptation of who we choose to be, however as spoken the decisions made and action taken, will determine who wins the war. The body itself is a representation of the spoils of war. (2:7) This is the war inside so I believe that, if people spent more time internally balancing and fighting the war within, then there would undoubtedly be less physical was in the world itself. (2:8) History has shown us that the warrior is not always meant to be the driver in all day-to-day life only a designated driver to the chief. However, the chief must know when to turn over the wheel so purpose may be served when the time comes. (2:9) They must balance each other.

The Book of Sacrifice

Sacrifice: The offering of something precious Deity: To offer up or kill for a purpose: To accept the loss or destruction of, for a end cause or ideal.

Chapter 1

(1:1) When we hear the word sacrifice, these days we automatically think of the negative stigma that has over generations been attached to the word itself. (1:2) Most perceive sacrifice to be a negative thing because of the acts that have been committed in association with the ideal of what sacrifice truly means. (1.3) Truth is sacrifice is more positive than anything. regardless of if it calls for the separation of or destruction of one thing it's still done, in the belief of something positive occurring after the sacrifice itself is made. (1:4) sacrifice Indeed has two sides as all things do on one end. It would be a positive impact on the other end, there will be a negative, or at least the appearance of a negative. (1:5) For the sacrifices the act will be done in attempts to bring a positive outcome, while for the sacrifice, whether it be a person, place or thing, the act will bring or appear to bring forth a negative effect. (1:6) In ancient history as well as present we've read of various sacrifices which were and are on a day-to-day basis by all, these acts range from large to small and need not much explaining to understand. (1:7) However, the most important and life altering sacrifices often involve people. (1:8) A human sacrifice! As described in many religious texts, people offered their lives or the lives of others, in hopes of bringing some type of positive desired result. (1:9) As a universal sacrifice, I believe that to sacrifice another life for the benefit for the benefit of one's own desire can never truly be justified! I believe the only way the sacrifice of life can be deemed just is when is when it's done to help to save or benefit another or others and that the sacrifice itself can only be by the one who will suffer physically. (1:10) Anyone other than the one who will suffer to make that decision. I believe it will be without a doubt a murder! (1:16) Forcing Physical separation and distance after an internal sacrifice is necessary, because one must get used to the lining without that person, place, or thing. (1:17) The process of grief could be harder in the sense that you would be aware that the person will still be alive where as in the physical sacrifices, the person would be dead and unable to be brought back which forces you to move o on in a different manner. (1:18) There will be days where you think of a loved one who is physically dead and the love you held and still have for them will cause you to wish you could bring them back. (1.19) There will also be days where you think of the loved one you sacrificed internally and the love that you had or still have for that loved one will cause you to question killing them off. (1:20) This can cause you to doubt your decision, ultimately causing you to continually consider amending the relationship even when you been shown it must stay buried. (1:21) This is the distinction between the two that is why one is harder than the other. Because one you actually have the power to bring them back from the dead. The other you don't. This is why one takes more strength than the other, even though they both take strength to accept in their own respects.

Chapter 2

(2:1) The beauty of the non-physical sacrifice, is that sometimes, it can be exactly what is necessary to begin to heal not only the sacrifice themselves but can also potentially help the sacrifice but can also by forcing them to take accountability for their ways and actions and using that to fuel to fuel change in their own. (2:2) For the reason who is killed off that separation can affect them sometimes so deeply that it can cause them to re-evaluate the way they are a person. (2:3) It can make them want to change and can also believe as a purgatory of sorts where they take the time to re-construct themselves from the inside out, so that one day if their loved one who killed them off, ever so chose to bring them back to life than they would be the version of themselves needed in order for the relationship between the two to be as healthy and positive as possible.

(2:4) Sacrificing someone internally, rather than physically, leaves a chance for a future relationship, if so, chosen by the one who's called to make the sacrifice, but also leaves room for the sacrificed to have a future themselves and a chance to actually change for the better. Even if that means they never get a second chance at life with their loved ones, they still get a chance to make up for it with future precautions, it's all determined by if they use their time in purgatory to change for the better. (If they remain the same selfish individual that caused them to be killed off in the first place, then that's solely on them. (2:6) Either way, if they change for the better while in purgatory, and the one who had to initiate the sacrifice heals themselves to a better place while in their grieving process, then you never know what may happen. Maybe, the universe will allow them an opportunity at a new relationship, with a new dynamic, healthier, respectfulness with the necessary boundaries set in place to make the relationship itself more positive in nature. (2:7) If the time in grieving and purgatory doesn't cause one to heal or change for the better than at least the sacrifice knows that they made the right decision and they are freed from negative impacts of the relationship.

(2:8) I believe there are internal sacrifices that need to be made in each of our lives. (2:9) In order to make them, we need only to look at the people in our lives, we must first set aside the blinding love that we have for them, second really analyze the ways their presence in our lives impact us to judge if no more negatively than then the third find the strength to take action no matter how much it hurts.

The Book Of Karma

Karma: The force generated by a person's actions in this as well as past existences.

Chapter 1

(1:1) Karma has always had the simplest basic explanation of "one reaps what they sow" (1:2) That if one does bad things then bad things will be done to them or possibly the closet to them. (1:3) Also, that if they do good things, then good things will come back to them as a reward. This concept is simply accepted as the basis of how karma works. (1:4) As a universal I believe the idea of Karma to be a bit deeper. I focus more on the dimension and believe that it plays a larger role than the physical dimension which is the dimension of their intention. (1:5) I believe that a person's intention is what ultimately gets judged by the universe as opposed to the physical action taken itself.

(1:6) I understand that there are times in life where one does right things for the wrong reasons. Just as there will also be times when one does the wrong thing for the right reason. (1:7) At any given time one may do something that hurts or harms another but only with the intention of protecting or preserving their own life or safety. (1:8) If their intent is never ill to begin with how or why could they be punished by the universe. (1:9) However I do believe that if one does wrong with an all intention purpose the return of their karma will be negative in nature without a doubt, it's their intention that makes the difference (1:10) Karma may not always be returned in an instant, but I believe its undoubtedly always a sure thing. (1:11) I also believe that karma doesn't always go back around directly to the person who committed the karmic deed as deserved. Instead, it may come back and touch someone close to them. (1:12) I believe they won't always acknowledge the feeling of the connection between what they did and how the karma came back around. But those with a certain level of awareness, I believe will always make that connection whether they chose to accept it in their heart or not. I understand the feeling of guilt can make you choose to accept it in their hearts or not. Hard to just to try and justify to ease their soul.

(1:13) I believe that one intention is what feeling is in their heart at the time of the act. (1:14) I believe the heart is what the universe listens to. (1:15) I understand there are plenty of people who try to manipulate good karma to themselves, but they don't understand that you cannot manipulate the universe. (1:16) People often do things with their intentions set on getting a form of good karma in return. In this act I know at times their intentions are selfish an immature. I believe and I stand firm in the pureness of the heart, knowing that will, ultimately in return get them a blessing they deserve in some form. (1:17) One shouldn't seek a reward, even being aware that a reward of good karma in some form usually follows. You can't fool the universe. (1:18) I believe one cannot take another life without an intentional purpose within the false thought that all they have to do to be forgiven by their creator is go to church and ask for forgiveness. (1:19) As a universal, I believe that, the universe gave them the ability to think, so there will never be a way to out think the universe in anything! (1:20) I believe that someone in that situation should understand that they did such a wrong with all ill intentional purposes, then the only way they will ever have a true chance at forgiveness is if the remorse for the act itself come from the heart not the brain. (1:21) If one doesn't understand this then their karma will surely walk, just paces behind them forever, if need be, to reach out and touch them in whatever way or whatever time the universe sees fit.

Chapter 2

(2:1) Sometimes it's a case where one may see another do the wrong thing with ill intent or better yet someone will do them wrong, with all intentional purpose and in return the affected will often call on the universe to deliver the karma to that person so that they may see that offender suffer how they suffered or may be worst

(2:2) As a universal I understand that even if you are done wrong, it can't be made right by you sending ill intent back at the person. (2:3) A universal must trust that the universe will honor the karma at the time of its own karmic clock. They also must accept that they might not be around to see if it come back full circle but must still trust that it will. (2:4) If they ever decide to take the karmic clock into their own hands out of pure impatience, they must be aware that they assume the risk of potentially being put in a position to be calling onto the universe may not be as easily forgiving because retaliation itself is a different beast of its own. (2:5) Retaliation signifies that one wants to create their own punishment for the offense brought upon them and the reality is, it's not up to them to give that judgement even though they have the ability. (2:6) It's no easy feat, but faith, patience, and forgiveness sometimes is the safest road to take. (2:7) However if one is truly willing to take whatever consequences may come when that karmic clock tick then, and stand strong with the belief from within that they did what's right, then however harsh the consequences may be for acting on their time of the universe with that gives them the strength to get through.

The Book Of Meditation

Meditate: To muse over: To contemplate or to ponder: to engage in deep mental exercise directed toward a heightened level of spiritual awareness.

Chapter 1

(1:1) Known to me as their medicine of the mind, the body, meditation's sole purpose I believe is to calm one mental bring about to a sense of inner peace. That inner peace, I believe is unattainable while one dwells in the chaos of thought. (1:3) One must understand, there is no one way to meditate! I believe a universality to meditation that Ables one to do so according to the comfortability to their own specific body and their own specific understanding, which is contrary to popular practices used by the masses. (1:4) I believe there is no specific way that one must align their body. Instead, I believe one must align their body. Instead, I believe they may position themselves in whatever bodily position they choose to provide their body the comfort of relaxation necessary to even begin the inner journey to becoming one with peace itself. (1:5) Peace resides in a universe completely sperate of thought! (1:6) I believe one cannot calm the physical body. Instead, can calm the internal body, then in doing so, the physical body itself will be realized to not exist once or if they reach the state of peace.

(1:7) I believe there are three important things one must put at the forefront of one's mind when seeking to feel the nirvana peace of meditation. One they must set their intentions on meditation not sleep or est. (1:8) Second, they must open their third eye by the way of closing the curtains of the two eyes the perceive life through. Upon closing the eyelids, I believe one will be instantly entered into the vision of the third eye which is one vision on abyss! This abyss, I believe internally transpires on to a place far beyond stars and planets galaxies. There are no ceilings, no walls, just endless space. An abyss of darkness as far as their eye can see. (1:9) Understand that just because one's eye lids are shut physically doesn't mean that their eyes themselves are actually closed. (1:10) I believe huma eye can't physically close, so instead one must see that their vision is still crystal clear, just in an internal reality that's majestic to an unfathomable extent. This vision, though restricted externally to a wall of darkness, can see far and deep into the world of the abyss

(1.11) The second thing I believe one must do, which is most pivotal, divorce themselves from all though to let the feelings of intuition guide them deep into the abyss.

(1:12) They seek it all beyond thought one traveling through space seemingly headed to an unknown somewhere where nothing exists except feeling of peace itself. As one travels deeper into the abyss of darkness, the thought of one's mind triggered by life experiences and emotions will begin to shoot any which way from every direction as does comets and asteroids in the deep darkness of space but still they must let the thoughts pass with the understanding that the thoughts can only clash if you entertain them. (1:13) One instead must let the power of intuition keep them focused and free enough to just let the thought pass as they come, as do asteroids in space when kept away or destroyed by atmosphere energy which exist unseen in all that lives. The journey through the deep darkness into peace may take quite some time to reach depending on how heavily the mind weighs on one at any given time. However, with time, pain and patience one may surely reach them if their intention is set purely inside their heart.

(1:14) The Universe is known to send the colorful light s of vision deep in that dark space, and one's conscience will be fully intact when they experience some form message transmitted through the universe from some pastime present time e or time that may come in the near future. One will seemingly feel as though they were delivered from a trans when their third eye closes and their two eyelids reopen. In this reality, the reality of the third eye is where the visions of the prophet's dwell. (1:15) Deep in the unknown where no one knows where they came from or returned to, their still accessible to anyone who seeks their enlightenment just as long as their intent is pure and they have the patience and consistency it takes for the universe to slowly let them into the world of the unknown, where anything is possible, everything seems unreal, but all that takes place is actually occurring and can be felt physically.

The Book of Medicine

Medicine: A substance or preparation used in treating disease: A science and art dealing with the prevention, alleviation and cure of disease for the millennium.

Chapter 1

(1:1) There have always been ways in which humans have found vast remedies to help heal the body of ailments. These remedies were born of natural cures found in nature such as herbs and different plants found growing from the earth which were boiled into water and consumed or at times placed directly onto the skin or wound to help cure. (1:2) As humas evolved, mentally as did the ways in which medicine was both invented and administered. Now over the generations of medicines evolution, there seems to have been created a "cure" for almost everything one may suffer from both physically and mentally. (1:3) While medicine may be the answer in more cases than not, one must understand as a universal that medicine isn't always something to be put in our bodies but is also to just be put into the mind. Not by needles or tea but by voice. (1:4) One must remember, the purpose of medicine is to heal one who is in some way suffering, and now, more than ever, the suffering of the mind is at an all-time high. (1:5) While medicine that is suggested for a mental illness may be the answer for one who suffers doesn't mean that the same should be said for all those who suffer. As humans one must understand that all humans suffer mentally in some way, or on some level. (1:6) In determining the level of severity, one must use the natural medicine of words. One must talk to the other who is in need of healing to truly get an understanding of what the best course of action should be taken to help heal the individual because now days, the mistake of a misdiagnosis of mental health issue is all too occurring. (1:7) Too commonly do the people of science seek to prescribe something for someone to ingest or inject not realizing that the long-term effects may in fact be causing more mental illness than healing., while healing one part of the mind they are in unison destroying a part of one's soul ultimately taking away a separate part of what makes them, them as an individual.

(1:8) Sometimes more than one, one just may need to be heard to be touched and acknowledged in a safe environment where they don't have to fear being misdiagnosed for saying the wrong thing, or the right thing the wrong way.

(1:9) Mental issues aren't always easy to articulate, and in these days that inability to articulate one's own state of mind or state of feeling can cause one to be taken to a place or institution they may in fact never return from. Even more so, in some cases they may return physically, but the one thing they needed the help healing, which is their mental, can at times actually never be present again as was before seeking the help. (1:10) Post admittance into these institutions their minds can be so far drained, in the ocean of medication their often led to by the people of science. (1:11) These people are often what I call mind murderers. They, are human, so they aren't all knowing. This means, they're not always right. Some of them not even fit as a person to be in the position to make any form of diagnosis or determination over other individual's life. (1:12) Others, as well are often just deceitful, profit minded beings of misconduct, that went to school to learn the words that get them the title and white cloth of a "Doctor."

(1:13) As a universal we must, restore back to the medicine of conversation. Extensive therapy alone, at times may be all that's needed to help heal the mind, so being taught alternatives to replace medication, such as using words (therapy) and even more advanced healing which uses no words at all once the way is taught, (meditation) then an individual may see for themselves that medication may've never been, nor will ever be a safe way for them themselves to heal mentally as an individual.

(1:14) People of science don't always remember that some minds are more fragile than others and in turn need more attention and treatment than others. However, the risky side effects of some medications of the people of science aren't always the solution. At times the things prescribed by the people of science can create in one an illness at the false pretense of healing another. (1:15) People of science stick to what they can see, what's physical, while medicine like meditation itself doesn't at all depend on what is seen physically but believed to be felt mentally on a more internal level.

(1:16) As a universal one must understand and believe that just a simple conversation can be a form of medicine, or a simple touch may heal a person internally. Things like faith, can heal, calling on a force greater than oneself through prayer can heal wholly or be medication to be used on at will whenever internal symptoms occur. (1:17) Shamas, sorcerers, witches and other holistic healers have forever been demonized by the people of science, and the cases even killed, but one must acknowledge that it was for their ability to call on a force greater than a doctor's prescription.

(1:18) Admittingly, they were successful in their ability to heal the sick or suffering, from both physical as well as mental ailments and in some cases being brought back from death itself, but such a power in this physical world of man science can't come from a source that exists in the realm of the unfathomable. Doctors will not allow it! (1:19) This realm is ethereal as well as physical, but its only accessible to those who believe that this unseen energy exists to begin with. (1:20) There is an unlimited source of healing power present that trumps the bottles and needles of sciences medicine cabinet on its darkest day, but Medicine exists in various forms all around us.

(1:21) As a universal we must remain aware that the most powerful medicines come from within us. A simple word, a simple touch a smile belief can be all the medication that will ever be needed.

The Book Of Energy

Energy: Vigorous action: A fundamental entity of nature: usable power such as heat or electricity:

Chapter 1

(1:1) As a universal, the key to understanding ourselves as beings we must simply understand that while we do have bodies and we do exist in a physical world, however, we ourselves are not the body of flesh itself. The body, which is just a vessel, can be discarded at any moment and we ourselves would still live on in our true form.

(1:2) We are the energy inside those powers the body and all of its complex components of functionality. Quite simply, we are energy. We ourselves, are nothing more than the bodies unseen battery.

(1:3) Comprised of two sides, we are both the positive charge, as well as the negative charge of energy that makes us whole, the body itself acts more of a ground. Just as a battery cannot consist of two positive charges, nor can it consist of two negative charges, we ourselves can consist of all positive energy or all negative energy. Even if one chooses to produce more positive energy, they still have negative energy that dwells in there being, just as someone who produces all negative energy, they still have positive energy that dwells in their being. It's just one's state of being that influences the kind of energy one puts in the universe. (1:4) It lies within their resting intention. Just as one has a resting heartbeat, one has a resting vibration that emits into the universe via their aura. Their resting vibration is determined by the state of one's internal balance, as well as their overall state of mind. (1:5) That inner intention produces coinciding energy that surrounds the person body like an unseen force. That unseen force of energy, if it is unbalanced and tilted more to negative vibration will ultimately be resisted and avoided but one who's vibration is balanced more toward the positive side of energy. (1:6) Usually people who [practice emitting purely positive energy, keep away from those who have a negative energy emitting from within them because the two forms of energy are like backward magnets trying to interlock! They only work in a balanced state, and when kept at a certain distance. Although they may both be energy, they never touch physically, they instead only get close enough for purposed friction. (1:7) Positive energy attracts positive energy, negative energy attracts negative energy, and the same could be said about that attracting energy manifesting respective events and circumstances in life that coincided with those merging forces.

(1:8) As a universal, one must understand that sometimes a person's negative energy may only be coming from a place of hurt or some other form of internal pain so it's sometimes an opportunity to find a way to help bring that person out of that place of negativity and help them cross over into a state of positivity, or at the very least, to a place of healthy balance. (1:9) Negative intention creates negative energy on an internal level, and negative energy on an internal level can then create negative occurrences in one's life on a physical level. Such is a domino effect. Positive intention creates positive energy on an internal level. Positive intention creates a positive energy on an internal level creates positive occurrences in one life on a physical level. Hence, you get back what you put in the universe. (1:10) The Universe is a place full of both positive and negative energy as well as positive and negative occurrences. There will always be things that happen that will be viewed as and felt as bad, just as there will always be things that are seen as and felt as good, even if these occurrences are only feelings and perspectives themselves and not truths of occurrence itself!

(1:11) Polarity is necessary. For without it, how will we, not only understand the journey of finding balance internally and externally, but how will we fully understand, not just life within the universe, but the life of the Universe itself? (1:12) If negativity serves a purpose in life that's needed to bring forth the positivity of understanding, then how long should one view negativity as negative? Why can't negative simply be viewed just as just necessary? After all, such is its true essence. If it is necessary for negative things in life to happen to understand or appreciate the positive things, then why demonize negativity just for doing as it was designed to do in the first place? (1:13) Why condemn the darkness for being dark when the purpose of the darkness was and is to help bring understanding and appreciation oft of the light? We must understand balance.

Why condemn weakness if its purpose is to help one understand and appreciate the power and purpose of strength. Why condemn the struggle for being hard to get through and overcome, when its purpose is to bring understanding and appreciation to prosperity? (1:14) The universe made no mistakes in the beginning when establishing the laws of the land. Just because negative things happen and we can't understand why or agree with why because of the negative ways it may affect us, doesn't mean that there wasn't a hidden positive reason or meaning behind it. Theres always plenty positivity to be found in midst of the negative situations we just close ourselves off to them because we don't like the happening itself.

(1:15) If and when somethings meant for one to understand, then they will understand what is meant for them to understand. Not a day sooner or a day later. Even still, if they never find understanding, that still doesn't mean there wasn't purpose behind it. It instead could just means that it wasn't meant for them to understand!

(1:16) Some things are only known to the Universe and we will never be in such a position to question or demand answers, so we must learn to find peace through acceptance so that we don't let negative events of one day of the past, become the present, in everyday of our future. (1:18) The dwelling of negative energy exists on the left side of the body, just as a negative charge exist on the left side of electricity. Examine a battery. The symbol of negative is on the left side and the positive is on the right. (1:19) We as people are the same and we subconsciously validate this with sayings and phases like "Everything just went left", "No man left behind." "It just came out of left field, so on and so forth. (1:20) Equivalently, the right is no different and we subconsciously validate the same way with sayings and phrases like "Everything is all alright" "That was the right thing to do/ That wasn't right." "In the right state of mind"., and so on and so forth. (1:21) As a Universal, one must understand that, this is no coincidence. Instead, this is more like a subconscious knowing!

The Book Of Language

Language: The words, there pronunciation and the methods of combining them used and understood by a community: Form or style of verbal expression: System of signs, symbols, and rules for using them to carry information.

Chapter 1

(1:1) Since the beginning of human kind the act of communication has evolved through the evolution of the human race. From grunts, mumbles, roars and cries, to words phrases and prolonged sentences spoken. However, regardless of what tongue one may speak in throughout the different locations of the world, as a universal one must know the language of the Universe. This language isn't of spoken word but yet and still understood and felt by all. This Language is action!

(1:2) Action, first is the word spoken. Discernment, second is the feeling brought about after the words of action to be processed to determine what the voice of action is attempting to say. (1:3) These two elements are a Universals language. A Universal doesn't rely on what is spoken from the mouth itself, but rather instead relies on what they can see with their eye first, then second or usually simultaneously what they discern after or amidst the occurrence of action. Truth for a universal, boils down to what's done and what's felt while what's being done has come to pass.

(1:4) It is action that speaks the most understandable words. Feelings are what then follows to determine the intention behind the action itself. The second component is where one could easily be just as confused as listening to someone speak in a foreign tongue because one's intentions behind their actions aren't always aligned with what they physically do themselves action wise.

(1:5) When a Universal listens to one's action, which could very well be viewed as a foreign tongue because intention isn't always initially clear just as slurred words from physical speech aren't always initially understandable, it's what is discerned by the one who attempts to interpret, that will make the action realistically comprehendible.

In attempts to understand the action one may use the mind but in attempts to understand the intention of the action the listener must rely on the intuition/ discernment to gauge the sincerity or deception that usually dwells in the subtext within the action.

(1:6) Sincerity and deception both produce energy that speaks directly to a Universal. A man encounters a beast in the wild. Man's intention is to trap in attempts to consume. The beast intention is to search for food, both to feed themselves or their families. The man retrieves a source of bait and uses the action of kneeling in a non-threatening manner and extending the bait in his palm in the appearance of an offering to the beast what he is sure it seeks. The beast sees the act and although it perceives the action to be an invitation. It relies on its instinct of discernment to feel out the intention behind the action of the man, for it can feel the intention of the deceiver in the air so it weighs out the risk of accepting or rejection.

(1:7) The invitation, no words need be spoken because they speak different tongues. However, it is both elements of the universal that are being used by the two to communicate with one another. In the encounter, if the man has mastered the art of deception by his intention to a level that puts the beast in a false sense of security, then he may very well prevail if he can cause the beast to set aside its instinct and trust in the invitation. The beast, depending how hungry it may be, may inwardly debate while inching closer, but if he sticks to its instinct of discernment and the deceiver releases the slightest bit of dark energy by way of intention then the beast will feel it and subsequently flee.

(1:8) A universal must understand that we all have the same instinct within, as does all beasts, and we all must rely heavily on it to guide us through life. Although action is a component of the universal language one must not forget that actions can deceive the mind, so every positive action may not be done out of positive intention. A deceiver prays on an impressionable mind and uses it to get what they want out of those they encounter all the while appearing at face value to be a loved one or a Alli.

(1:9) Action isn't always done in sincerity, so the discernment is the only defense a Universal can and must rely on to keep themselves from being trapped, misused or abused for trusting purely action and action alone. Intention is everything!

(1:10) A bully may go around imposing offensively aggressive actions towards those around them, but those same aggressive and offensive actions may only be done as a defense mechanism to protect the exposing of the bully's cowardice. The action may appear to make them seem to be dominant, but the inner intention behind it all is to deceive. A universal who's in tune with their instinct of discernment will be able to feel the false energy of the actions done to conclude that the bully isn't what it is perceived to be, there for they will have confidence and strength to stand up to the bully and force them to expose their true self, or if they flat outright know their stronger, they can stand up to the bully all the same.

(1:11) While the language of the universe is easier to understand than words because words aren't easy for all to comprehend when a foreign tongue is applied or a smooth-talking liar is present, just remember, that action is the most understanding form of communication. Remember that all action isn't genuine so one must implement the instinct discernment to determine sincerity or deception. Master this language and you can always be in tune with what's truly being spoken…Without even having to speak one word if you choose not to.

The Book Of Stars

Star: A celestial body that appears as a fixed point of light: A body that is gaseous, self-luminous and of great mass: the sun:

Chapter 1

(1:1) The stars of the nights sky has always been my biggest intrigue. When I look at the infinite above and beyond. (1:2) They themselves often raise more questions than answers but have also been used as solutions to some of the problems of humanity.

(1:3) Generations before the invention of the compass indigenous people looked to the stars to help guide the as they navigated themselves throughout the land and the waters. Navigators of the past looked to the stars raised their hand and pinpointed their own location, as well as looked to the earth's stars (that's the sun) to even estimate the time of day, from sun rise to sun set.

(1:4) I understand galaxies create stars, stars themselves create planets, and planets create life. Life then grows to create more life before death so that the cycle may continue.

(1:5) I understand that knowing this one must look to the stars and understand that each star, just as the star humanity calls the sun, gives life to the planets within its atmosphere. Without a star's presence planets would be unable to sustain not only life upon it, but also life without it itself. (1:6) Therefore, all planets need a healthy balance of sustained from the star who orbit they occupy. (1:7) I truly believe that the stars are where we all came from, and in the end it's back to the stars we will return. (1:8) The inner light and darkness of our own being is given life by the gas and fire that is the star itself. It is when we and our ancestors were sent from to take our place on the planet on this land. It is the home of my celestial bloodline and the root of the home tree of my people. (1:9) As a seeker I looked to the stars to find which shining light it is that I came from to truly understand myself on a cosmic itinerary level. (1:10) I believe different stars' systems breed different people more importantly, I truly believe that although the essence of our being comes from the stars, we ourselves still metaphorically play the role of a star in our own individual lives as humans. (1:11) I believe that a flame from the star in which I came from burns within me giving me the energy to then sustain and support the lives of those who are in my life, this would be equivalent to the planets that orbit a star. (1:12) I believe I am metaphorically a star! The planet in my solar system is metaphoric to my life! (1:13) Outer space is metaphorically the world I live in and comets and asteroids are metaphoric to the chaos and turmoil in my life my trial tribulations.

(1:14) It is up to me to determine the healthy the healthy dose of balance each person needs from me to not only help them help themselves to sustain and progress, but to also help me maintain the energy it takes to do the same for all other people (planets) that are in your orbit.

(1:15) In your solar system, there must always be a healthy sense of space and balance so that there will be no chaos amongst those who have a place in your life. This way people don't cause more turmoil in your orbit which is turmoil in your life. (1:16) There will always be people's places and events that will metaphorically play the role of asteroids that pass through your solar system and cause damage offsetting the balance such is the nature of life. Those times, however, are just times one must put in the work to ensure that all is rebalanced and peaceful once again. (1:17) The turmoil amongst those in your life can be prevented by determining which people get metaphorically placed on which planet within your solar system: As the stars, you get to decide how many people have a place in your life, just a star decides how many planets have a place within their orbit. (1:18) You as the star can push people out just as the star can Push a planet out of its orbit. You have the power! Timing is the key, and the love you may have for someone can cause you to take longer to push them out or create the distance needed to initiate the process but as long as you remain aware of the turmoil they carry with them, you must gradually work toward slowly pushing them out if not all together then at least reprojecting to a place where they don't get as much energy from you as the star, the sun (1:19) Some people have more people involved in their lives just as some stars have more planets in their orbit, this is usually determined big of a person or star they are. The bigger the star they are the stronger the influence or gravitational pull, the stronger the influence or gravitational pull the more responsibility, the more responsibility, the greater the dependability of those impacted by them and the greater the number of dependents, come the greater need for balance and order in one life and in a star's orbit! (1:20) Hence, one can decide how many people they have the strength to support, just as a star can, and the people in their lives need too prioritized and placed on whatever planet the strs see fit.

(1:21) Say you as a star decides to set a total of five planets I your solar system. The first being planet household family, second being planet family, the third being planet third, and forth being planet follower. This would help with the first initial placement of people in one's solar system.

Chapter 2

(2:1) Understand that as he star you can set as many as necessary and name them as you please for it is your solar system, but the people most directly impacted by your energy should always be place on the 1st planet Because those are the people most closet to you. (2:2) Usually the spouse and the children as time passes and the planes of people orbit around you as the sun, relationships are prone to change, this placement on planets should change as well. Not out of anything personal but just for the sake of peace and balance. (2:3) Someone from planet follower may make it to planet friend, thus making it closer to you a star. Someone from planet friend may make it to planet family as friend often grow to be just as close as a family member, sometimes even closer because sometimes family isn't just the bloodline it's a bond. (2:4) Fittingly someone from planet family mat deserve to be moved backwards to planet friend, not because there's no longer a relation to them by blood but because they need to place at a further distance so that order and balance may continue throughout your orbit. (2:5) As said, the number of names of planets can be whatever one chooses as the star. There can be planet coworker, planet friends' friend, planet stranger, planet exile, and so on and so forth. The key as the star is to always keep track of people's placement because the closer, they are to you determines how much chaos they could potentially cause to you and those closest to you. (2:6) One should remember that the star gets life by supporting the lives they surround it. Just as people get energy from people in their lives. (2:7) Thery feed each other, they motivate each other to do more, to be more, to go above and beyond devoting all that they are a star to all that the people or planets may need.

(2:8) Remember, the people closest to you as the star are representation of the closet planet to you in your solar system because they are the most directly impacted by your radiation, which is synonymous to your energy. (2:9) You give them life, or you drain them of life. (2:10) However, the most important thing one must understand and respect is that they as the star in your solar system the planets revolve around you still you have to remember to respect the fact that simultaneously living on the first planet in their own solar system. (2:11) Everyone is a star in their own solar system, and one must simultaneously balance living on a planet in the universes of those closest to them while also being the star in their own lives. Having to find such a balance of those two facets of existing is what speaks to the mechanism of the cosmos. (2:12) The star that guides the stars guide, is the star that all-stars should follow. (2:13) This star will never lead one astray. This star, the brightest star in the night sky. The star that other star's look to for a sense of direction in life and in nature. (2:14) The birthplace of many star's that were born to lead those in their lives who looked to them. (2:15) The North star.

(2:16) The star in which I believe to be sent from.

The Book of DNA

DNA: Any various nucleic acids that are usually the molecular based of hereditary and located especially in cell nuclei.

Chapter 1

(1:1) One must know their DNA At some point in their adult life, they should seek to trace it as far back in its origins as possible on both paternal sides to get a sense of who they are as a person and why they are the way they are as a human being. This can also help explain why they develop certain behaviors, thinking patterns and even sicknesses.

(1:2) DNA is the most accurate form of identification because one can't deny the bloodline they derived from. Your DNA is one of one. Even if born with a twin. Still, there are traces of the ancestors borne of the bloodline of your lineage that will forever linger with you whether one chooses to accept it or not, believe it or not. (1:2) As a universal one must understand that DNA not only has the ability to enable one to trace backwards in their own bloodlines history, It also gives one the ability to carry the spirit of their predecessors within them. It allows on to be protected by their unseen presence at times of danger, as well as be comforted and validated by them in times of love and comfortability. (1:3) It allows one direct access to speak with them at any and all times they choose to just as long as they are one, aware, and two, that they in their heart believe.

(1:4) Even if one doesn't know which ancestor they themselves connected with the deepest, they can still, without an lucid visual, acknowledge the ancestors presence. Through the act of this simple yet complex acknowledgment, their connection will grow stronger and ultimately enable your ancestors to draw closer to you to protect and guide you more, thus strengthen your presence. They themselves are the angles acknowledged by many different cultures.

(1:5) They may never be seen physically, however, to a Universal, they will always be felt because they will forever remain present in spirit. The spirit of their essence still lives wherever even a trace of their blood flows, and therefor they will forever be present and flowing through your veins, thus giving you strength to keep pushing when the struggles of life become a bit much to carry alone. (1:6) They will always and forever, whether your aware or not, be allowed to step in to aid one to safety and guide, sometimes even flat out carry you through times of darkness and turmoil.

All one must do is simply believe they are present, that even though they aren't seen by the eye their presence is felt by the body.

(1:7) Loved ones never truly leave, instead they just cross over to the unseen world after discarding their vessel. A universal must understand however, that the world of the unseen is still accessible through feeling. Connection to loved ones who crossed over to the unseen may be accessed through the connection of DNA that flows in one's bloodstream or by the connection developed through the bond established in imprinting of the two spirits just the same as DNA does one with the entire bloodline of their heritage. This allows the imprinted to be accessible just as ancestors and blood relatives that have crossed over to the unseen world. (1:8)

A grandmother who has been active enough to know a lot of the family members that their children or grandchildren have never met, may say you remind me of your aunt, uncle or cousin, and the children or grandchildren may not be able to fathom the statement.

This is because the grandmother, physically having that bond with the crossed over ancestor, sees that the spirit of that ancestor chose to live on as a part of that child or grandchild. If the child didn't have that physical bond, then mentally their mind wouldn't be able to connect to the statement having never saw or been in the presence of that ancestor. (1:9) The universe sends certain Ancestors to live on as a part of certain descendants for certain purposes only known to the ancestors. They get assignments and can interfere as offer as or as minimal as the universe allows them to and they're to follow these orders to the tee. (1:10) The blood that flows through that descendant is what allows the ancestor to forever assist their descendants for as long as the bloodline exists.

(1:11) This is why, a punishment centuries ago, one wouldn't just be punished as an individual, especially if sentenced to death for some unforgivable offense. They'd also be punished further more by getting their entire blood line wiped away from existence to ensure that the spirit of the accused may never exists again, even in spirit, within another that carries the DNA

(1:12) DNA lives forever. DNA is unshakeable, and burning the body and blood from existence, is the only way to truly rid the presence of an individual or an entire bloodline. Unless that is done, then the spirit of one's ancestors may live on and remain accessible, as the DNA will simply continue to multiply time and time again. (1:13) One child who possesses the DNA may carry the fat e of the entire ancestral tree by being the last of the bloodline. If they don't bear children, then the DNA line forever dies with them causing the entire tree to fall from the forest floor and sink back into the earth's womb.

The Book Of Free Will

Free Will: Voluntary choice or decision.

Chapter 1

(1:1) Since the beginning of time, there's always been a question raised throughout the different communities of believers/ religious groups that raise the debate of free will. Does a free spirit have free will? (1:2) Does one have the power to make their own decisions, henceforth forging their own path, subsequently leading them to their own individual purpose, cementing their own fate?

(1:3) Many believe in such a concept as free will. Where one does have the power to create their own destiny, while many others believe that there is a God of their own belief or understanding looking down on the world in control of all things that take place in the world. All the violence, as well as all the good. Many also believe that the story of our existence was all pre -written, so in essence, no matter what decisions we chose to make in life, whether their right or wrong, it was all predetermined for us to make because the story was already predetermined, henceforth, one had no control over what was already destined to occur.

(1:4) These two worldly views are exact opposites, but for the prewritten theory to be true, that would ultimately suggest that all humankind, in essence, are nothing more than mere robots experiencing a pre-programed existence controlled or governed by some unknown external writer responsible for the penmanship in our physical life cinematic unveiling. (1:5) As if life were a movie and we all were given a script of lines to recite/ intentionally improv, the worldly movie director/ curator gets to watch from above, below or wherever that place may be and be entertained 24/7, 365.

(1:6) Will one ever truly know the truth to the question of freewill? No! Does the true answer to the question really matter? I believe that answer is determined by who you ask. Me I've come to accept that there's beauty in the mystery, however I would want to know what level of control I myself have over my own existence! Still in the end, all that truly matters is what one truly believes for wishes for themselves and their own understanding. It's the individual's relationship and understanding of whatever God or source of power they seek strength and protection from that will determine what they will choose to believe in regards to the notion of freewill.

(1:7) Where does a Universal stand on the issue of free will? A universal understand it's creation on a level unfathomable to the human mind. Thereby, understanding the depth of the double-edged answer. Yes, the Universe gave all its creation the gift and burden of free will, yet also was able to prewrite the story of existence through the intuition of being all knowing, all seeing, and all feelings.

(1:8) The universe moves lifetimes and galaxies ahead of and beyond its creation, just as a player of the game of chess seeks to move a few moves ahead of their opponent. It's a micro image of the same instinct of the all-knowing, all seeing, and all feeling, of the universe, except that the universe is never wrong about its creations next decision as opposed to a player of chess may miscalculate or mis predict.

(1:9) The universe made all its creations and sent them out to the playground that is planet earth for all to live, learn, play, love, be hurt, recover, assist each other, bond, fight, so on and so forth, just as children do when taken to a playground by their parents who sit back and watch while their children interact with other children to build character and confidence. (1:10) The children are free to do as they so choose and as an overseer the Universe both simultaneously send tests to the children by way of interactions wit others as well as support by way of the ancestors and guides that dwell within and around these children whether known or unbeknownst to them, and even at times unbeknownst to the parents, who at many times arnt even paying attention from where they themselves may be sitting supposedly onlooking.

(1:11) Already able to anticipate the choices that will be made in advance, even without influence or intervening, the universe is able to put people, places and things in place to help all its children go through, get through, learn from and overcome all they may be called to endure in order for them to grow into whatever it's meant for them to become. Those same experiences of pressure and hardship in life are what ultimately mold one to become what they are destined to be. Still, at the beginning of the morning and the end of the day, it is their choice to fold or grow.

(1:12) Some are born into everything and more, while others are born into nothing at all, and others must fight for everything they acquire fighting the thoughts of the unfairness of a reality of inequality. Some are simply given all they desire.

(1:13) Some born into everything, eventually get to a place where they seek to go out on their own free will because they no longer want to feel the feeling of entitlement or the feeling of being controlled by the one that gives them all they desire. This makes them in return walk away from a life that's centered around what their giver needs and wants out of them as opposed to what they want out of life for themselves. (1:14) It takes independent strength for one to decide to leave a life of ease and accessibility for a life of uncertainty and struggle, but in the end, for those types of people, the feeling of internal freedom that comes with that decision usually is enough for them to know they made the right decision for themselves. These individual's undoubtedly have the strongest will power.

(1:15) Some are born into nothing and get to a place in life where they seek to go out on their own to earn for themselves. (1:16) Internally, they will no longer be able to accept a life of having nothing and being looked down upon by those who have, or being looked at as an equal to those who brought them into the life of not having but grew content and decided to accept the life of not having as a livable reality.

(1:17) It takes strength to desire not to accept contentment of the reality of poverty one may be born into, and off sheer will power, and ambition, work themselves into a position in life where they can have all they desire. This too requires an equal a power of will just a different motivator.

(1:18) Although at two different starting points, even two different sides of circumstance, the power of free will, in the end is what set the two on the same path, headed in the same destination, which is a path of Independence and not being content. (1:19) Regardless of what's chosen for one to do in their life time, the universe will ultimately put people places and things along the way in each's respective journey to both further, as well as hinder them depending on their decisions. (1:20) However, as a universal the most important thing to remember is the choice isn't made by the universe, it's instead only divinely anticipated. (1:21) The full power of free will itself, ultimately and undoubtedly resides in oneself! The Power is yours!

The Book Of Struggle

Struggle: Contest, strife, to make strenuous efforts against opposition. To proceed with difficulty or with great effort.

Chapter 1

(1:1) Many often point to the harsh struggles and misfortunes of life to raise the issue that there can't be such a thing as a god who sits in heaven watching down on all creation. Some argue, "If there was then how could he or she or they look on and allow all the bad things that take place to take place?" (1:2) How could God look on while people go homeless sleeping on the streets? How could God look on while children die before fully getting a chance to experience life? How could God look on while one steals from another, rapes another, tortures another and most extremely kill another. (1:3) How or why would or could God even create such experiences as struggle, strife, pain, heartache grief or any other experience that brings about a bad feeling or bad thoughts? Why can't the world just be all good?

(1:4) While these are fair questions for one to pose to themselves or to others, a universal must understand, that although the struggle is turbulent, sorrowful, painful, and may make one feel as though their walking in a trail of tears that last for years, the struggle is ultimately necessary, as ugly as it maybe it is undoubtedly essential in the balance of life.

(1:5) Without struggle, how else would one be able to not just appreciate prosperity when they overcome the struggle, but to have learned the lessons necessary to be able to sustain that prosperity long enough to subsequently create generational prosperity that can then be passed on when they themselves pass on. What better way to be motivated to evade the struggle by any means than to have had to experience the struggle in some form fashion.

(1:6) The struggle itself has many different faces because people struggle in many different forms and fashions. The same can be said about prosperity because it not just one way a person can be prosperous. There are both internal as well as external levels of both struggle and prosperity but at the beginning of the morning and the end of the day, the overcoming of struggle itself is what matters most.

(1:7) Overcoming whatever form of struggle that the universe might bestow upon one, no matter how hard, unfair, or unfathomable it maybe, should always remain the end goal, because although the struggle is a struggle, one mustn't forget that the struggle itself is necessary. So, struggle until you prosper!

(1:8) Struggle is the test. The struggle is the preparation. The struggle is meant to be heavy on the backs of those who are called to carry it. The heavier the load, the stronger one will be called on to be and those chosen with burdens of the heaviest loads must know that its simply because the universe has a lot of others whose lives will tie into and need help from you in some way or another. They are the strongest leaders. (1:9) They need the preparation because they will have much greater responsibilities than others and will be given the power to pull all those who are sent to them by the universe out of the struggle!

(1:10) Having had experienced severe struggle firsthand, one won't give back in an enabling way in the end because they were abundantly rewarded for enduring. They will instead, after overcoming, give back in a way that teaches that understanding that being able to bring another out of the struggle is the reward itself!

(1:11) Whether mental struggle, emotional struggle, social struggle, financial struggle, physical struggle. There will always be set in place the means for one to seek to make it to the other side of any respective struggle to make it to the promised land of prosperity. That statement goes to all forms of prosperity, Internal as well as external. (1:12) One can experience the struggle spiritually and seek the means to overcome their spiritual struggles if they choose. One can experience the struggle financially and seek the means to overcome their financial struggles. Roads to the other side of the struggle will forever be present. It's just up to the one who carries the load to keep pushing and not fall victim to the weight of the struggles, become complacent or accept the struggle as their forever reality. That decision to fold, would be not only accept failing the test of self, but it also is synonymous to giving up on all those who the universe was strengthening and grooming you to be responsible for helping guide when you finally were seen fit.

(1:13) Lot's give up just before they make it to the unseen and unknown finish line. They justify and take the victim stance. "It's the hand I was delt" is the cliché they adopt, figuring It's much easier to justify giving up, than continuing to keep fighting or holding onto the notion of keeping the faith. "The struggle too shall pass" is the thought that one should adopt while in the midst of struggle, even though it's easier said than done when you ultimately don't know exactly how long the struggle is meant to last.

(1:14) The greatest leaders are those who overcame the struggle, because in that experience, they acquired the power of compassion and understanding it takes to give them a certain perspective when it comes to seeing other people who may still be in it in some form, ultimately instilling within them a sense of sympathy that may cause them to help. (1:15) Still there are exceptions, because there will still be those who may come from the struggle, but still, knowing no one helped them when they needed help, they turn their backs against the world with an ignorance or arrogance that may in fact project heartlessness.

(1:16) If an employer who's wealthy and has been born into wealth therefore knowing nothing of financial struggle, was to employ another who comes from financial struggle, and is able to afford childcare to make it work. The Wealthy employer will lack the understanding of that dilemma because they would be unable to fathom not being able to pay a nanny due to rent and the power bill being more of a priority that month. In this scenario, the wealthy employer may then fire the employee.

(1:17) If one who experiences financial struggle and stays strong enough to reach prosperity there by acquiring the power of understanding and compassion was employed by another who is experiencing financial struggle and is unable to come into work because of childcare.

(1:18) This struggle experienced employer, instead of firing the employee, may even seek to find a way to help, not just because they know what it's like to struggle but also because they remember that the gift they were given after overcoming their own prosperity, was the ability to go any length they may be called to go in order to be there for one of those whose story was tied into their own and made more responsible for by the universe. (1:19) Just a long as their careful not to create a sense of entitlement.

(1:20) Experiencing struggles and overcoming them to a point that your able to bring another out of any form of struggle is the proof of prosperity. (1:21) Whether it be overcoming financial struggle then being put in a position to pull someone out of financial struggle. Whether its overcoming mental struggles to find the peace of mental balance to then help pull someone else out of their own mental struggle, or suffering spiritually, then overcoming to get to a place of internal peace that allows you to pay it forward and elevate someone else into a place of internal peace, a universal must never forget that the gift of prosperity was given to them by the universe, but the gift of prosperity is meant to be passed on. It's a gift meant to keep on giving.

Chapter 2

(2:1) Hard? Yes! Painful? Yes! Heavy on the shoulders? Yes! Hard to understand, therefore easy to question, yes. The struggle indeed is all these things. However, above all, the struggle is undoubtedly necessary! (2:2) It's the test that must be passed for one to compassionately uphold their oncoming responsibilities, and a universal understands that the only way to get through something is to actually go through something.

The Book Of God

God: The supreme reality; the being or beings worshipped as the creator or creators and rulers of the universe: A being, or object believed to have supernatural attributes and powers and require worship: A thing of supreme value: Extraordinarily attractive person or thing.

Chapter 1

(1:1) Who is God? What is God? Where is God? These are a few mysteries that can never be answered in a non-disputable way, therefore will forever remain unknown. (1:2) When it pertains to these mysteries of who or what God is or may be, one can only rely on what they themselves believe. Even still, it doesn't make what they choose to believe to be true. It just makes it true to that individual, which is all that matters, for they have the freedom to believe what they please.

(1:3) Some believe that there is a such thing as God. A God that's a Man, with a Son, with no Woman, nor daughter, and still singlehandedly responsible for all that exists. While others, believe that there were multiple God's whom are all responsible contributing in some form or fashion by playing their role in the overall creation of humankind. (1:4) Whether God of the Bible. Whether God of the Karahn. Whether the God's of Africa, The God's of Egypt, The God's of Olympus, the God's of India or Native Indians worship of the Great Spirit, the common theme of all the different belief systems is that God, without a doubt, is a living, external being. (1:5) Whether believed to be a man or believed to be a woman depends on who you ask and from cultural background or spiritual belief system, but what stands firm is that people believe that God is in fact acknowledged to be a living being. (1:6) The question is and has always been, what type of living being? Is he or she a living being like humans or a living being of a more supreme and supernatural reality!

(1:7) As a universal one must understand the answer is the more logical of the two perspectives, just with a deeper level of understanding that may've never been articulated in a way for one to fathom changing their perspective. (1:8) A universal understands that creation is a process involving multiple forces that work together in respective ways to serve a purpose in the creation of all humanity knows and sees. These forces together make God. (1:9) They are the powers that the universe consists of. God living in plain sight.

(1:10) A universal understands that everything that produces is a living being, not just humans, not just animals, not just plants. A universal understands that planets themselves are living beings. (1:11) The universe is one family of living things. These living things are responsible for the evolution of the universe itself and the life force of each God is represented in one of the four Elements of creation. Earth, Air, Water and Fire. Translation; Mother, Father, Daughter and Son…

The Book of Family

Family: A social unit usually consisting of one or two parents and their children. A group of individuals living under one roof under one head: A group of persons of common ancestry: A group related plant animals ranking in biological classification above a genius and above an order from infinite grand grands, or grandmothers, to grandfathers, mothers, fathers, brothers, sisters, daughters, sons, aunts, uncles, cousins all 1st, 2nd, and 3rd etc.

Chapter 1

(1:1) Families consist of these titles. All that are born take a place in this hierarchy. Whether a single mother with no other family alive brings forth a child or twins, these children would take place as the son or daughter as well as sister or brother, same as their mother has taken the place as daughter, maybe even sister and aunt. (1:2) Upon their arrival, multiple titles are bound to follow as families naturally multiply. Children grow on to become mothers and fathers, restarting for their children, the same process in which the parents themselves once experienced to ultimately continue the process therefore adding more titles to the parent's life and timeline such as grandparents. (1:3) Lastly and infinitely, is level of the Great Grands. This level of Supreme elder is where the Great doubles, triples, and compounds infinitely to extend to an infinity of Great.

(1:4) All families aren't in fact big; some instead are very small in comparison to others. Some are small due to the distance created by some form of dysfunction; therefore, many members are unknown.

(1:5) More times than none, these families usually only consisted of Parents and siblings. Outside of that there may be a Grandparent or two somewhere locally with maybe an extended cousin or two which may connect an Aunt Uncle and a few cousins. Overall, the family is still small as a whole.

(1:6) No matter the size of the family, one must accept that they themselves have no choice in the matter of what family their born into. Whatever situational disfunction or dynamic one is born into, one has no say in the blood that flows through their veins. It's what they will have to accept and eventually embrace as a part of their being, because it is responsible for the creation of their self.

(1:7) However, as a universal one must understand that a family is not limited to those that share the same Bloodline.

(1:8) The word family roots deeper than just a single tree. Family is understood to a universal to be not just the blood, but more so, the bond shared between people. These Bonds are in Spirit. (1:9) There are packs, pride, troupes, clans, colonies, that aren't all of the same blood, or at times not even the same species but can ultimately, all come together for some greater cause, thus forming a bond that eventually can bring them to feel for, and view one another as family. (1:10) As a universal, one must understand that's the same goes for humans when establishing a tribe. If the bond is there, which in many cases it does eventually formulate between two individual's or tribes then it's the family the potential for a spirit family to be established through pure bond. (1:11) These Spirit families often grow to be stronger as well as last longer than that of blood family because its these spirit families that are often brought together by purpose, so the individual's present often share the same beliefs and interest which makes the relationship feel more natural in essence. A Universal is aware that spirit is more organic that blood!

(1:12) As children, many may grow up in home elements that do so much harm to them physically; emotionally, mentally, socially and economically, that they long for the day when they come of age and have the ability to emancipate themselves from the family they were birthed into. (1:13) They may prefer the total destruction of and complete separation from these birth families, to in return create a family of their own, which would then give them the opportunity to recreate an experience of upbringing they'd prefer for their own children to experience while growing up rather than accepting the generational curses that often comes with birth families. (1:14) This decision gives their children, not just an advantage they themselves as the providing parent wish they had growing up but it will ultimately help their children grow up with a healthier example, and a better understanding of what family should look and feel like.

(1:15) While family is and should be held as most important to one in life, one must understand that, once one leaves the family they were born into, to create a family of their own by way of having children with a spouse starting their own household together, that family that is created by them and for them will then come to supersedes that of the family one was born in to.

(1:16) Families consist of people, people consist of flaws, and flaws amongst multiple people bring forth family issues and disfunction. These issues will often call for one to choose sides in disputes and bring resolve to the issues that may arise within the family; however, one must remember that their individual family presides over everything, so all decisions must be made in accordance to what's best for their own individual family when there's turmoil between their family and their birth family.

(1:17) One must understand that although harsh, the fact remains, that blood alone doesn't make you family, blood is just what makes one individual, or group to another. (1:18) The word family should be reserved exclusively for those that share the family bond that henceforth makes the love shared rise to the level of unconditional. A universal knows, strangers may grow to become more like brothers if the two are in alignment at the right time while, while blood brothers may grow apart eventually seeing each other as strangers.

(1:19) It all depends on, not just the outgrowing of the forced connection of relative's we try so hard to hold onto for the sake of siblinghood or family in general, but even more so, the likeness and the differences that establish the compatibility between respective people.

(1:20) This at times can bring forth jealousy and bitterness. Just because you share the same blood as another, it doesn't mean that they deserve to have a presence in the family you create for yourself after a certain point in life. This doesn't mean that you don't love them anymore, one just must learn to have the strength necessary to love from a distance so that the atmosphere in your individual family can remain at the peace of balance it will eventually be challenged to be kept at.

(1:21) Many times the birth family will come to be the subconscious (sometimes sadly the intentional) opposition of the self-created family and it will be up to you to fight the fight with no holding back to balance what you created for yourself, even if that means complete and total separation. No fucks given, I advise you cut off anyone and anything that disrupts the balance of your family. No Exceptions!

Chapter 2

(2:1) Often one will tolerate inconveniences, stagnation, derailments and stress all brought onto them purely because they were taught that family sticks together no matter what. This statement is only true to an extent of who you yourself truly hold in your heart as family and more importantly, who are the ones that show you that that sentiment is reciprocated enough in a tangible enough way for you to say they hold you in that they hold you in their heart in that same regard. (2:2) While one should always do what they can to help another family member if its within reason, they must understand that the rules change when one has a family of their own, so creating space between yourself and members of your born family will be paramount. This will be the only possible way for one to be truly present I every way possible for the family they create for themselves.

(2:3) To have the strength and energy to be all they need to be in their households, at times the distance that's created between people or relations is the only way one may have a shot at peace for them and the household, not out of a loss of love by necessity. This is how families fall into factions. Families within families, and if there is no matriarch or patriarch (usually a grandparent) to play the role as the glue or foundation any longer, these sub families often fall out, and eventually each child of the patriarch and the matriarch will take their individual families and become the foundation for theirs after separation and their children will grow and procreate until the title of, the new matriarch or patriarch in their subfamily.

(2:4) If they aren't close with their siblings, then each will respectfully falloff into their own sub family leaving any of their children to feel the effects of the distance put between siblings or cousins if they aren't of the age to keep in contact with their separated family themselves. This leads to the roles of the family members sometimes being filled by friends who eventually become more like family, or strangers who fill those voids to becomes more like blood family.

(2:5) Blood doesn't matter in the making of family, all that matters is that everyone shares the same bond and can maintain peace and balance even amidst differences in beliefs and opinions. If one can only contribute negativity, then distance may be the necessary if its outside the household, because once a household family is established, it supersedes all else. (2:6) Remember Family isn't Everything. It's Your Family that Everything!

Revelation of Genesis

(The First Family Of Creation)

Foreword;

Where does the word family originate from? What is the social order that humans understand family to be created from or made in the image of? To a Universal, the answer to this mystery is hinted in the christening as the title of whatever family comes to resides in the house is said to be the most powerful house in the United States. (The White House) This is no coincidence! Furthermore. The answer to this mystery is also is hinted in the christening of whatever family comes to reside at the head of (The Church).

A Universal is aware of why "The First Family" title is the highest title a whole family unit can be honored with and one must understand that this too is no coincidence. Compromised of the first mother, the first father, the first daughter and the first son. This is the family that together made it possible for all humankind to take its place as the grandchildren in the hierarchy.

What would Creation be without Life itself besides incomplete? 100% Responsible for all that is, still 0% responsible for all that live.

What would Life be without Creation itself besides incomplete? 100% responsible for all that live, still 0% responsible for all that is. TOGETHER THEY ARE GOD… (Bawnde Uni)

Chapter 2

(2:14) Seeing through this universal perspective, can one honestly still disagree that, together, the earth and the air are the first mother and the first father that began the universe. (2:15) Through dust and gas did they not together spark off all that the universe eventually became, and remain to this present? I believe that even the skeptic minds of the women and men of science. To dispute this understanding, they've been religion Faiths greatest opposition, in all history. Especially when it come to the holy Bible story of creation. In genesis. (2:16) the earth and the heavens the mother and the father, together God/ God of creation and life. What is the body which is the mother's first creation without life? When facing death does a paramedic does not turn into the first father, by wat of C.P.R. where on attempts to blow the breath of life back into the body? (2:17) If that fails do, they do not call the father for more assistance by way of an E.K.G machine when they then attempt to shock the light of life back into the body. (2:18) The first mother always calls on the first father who is he better half as she Is his. She is the brain while he is the Braun. She is thought while he is action. (2:20) After arranging everything necessary for the supernatural process of evolution to begin the first mother and father then brought forth their first and only children. (2:21) Their children carry on their mission, so they themselves, having laid down the foundation may observe the rest.

Chapter 3

(3:1) Only two children to ever exist! The first daughter and the first son. (3:2) Crated in the same image as their parents as opposites, so they were left and right. Brought forth by the below and the above tasked to have domination over all there is, over all that lives, so that they were.

(3:3) Just as I universal interpreters; genius (1:1) "As homage to the first mother and first father. I to as a universal interoperate homage being given to the first daughter and the first son in the same genesis, Chapter (1:27) So it says "Then God Said, " Let us make man in our image, according to our likeness: Let them have dominion over fish of the sea, over the birds of the air,over all the cattle, over all the earth, and over every creeping thing that creeps on the earth. (1:27) So God created man in his own image, in the image of God he created him; Male and female he created them: then God blessed them; and God said to them be fruitful and multiply.

(3:4) The Holy Bible calls for one to believe that there is one God, whom is man and has one child who is a man, and he alone created all there is in the universe. (3:5) A universal, is accepted and respected by those who accept this as their truth. The verse that I find hard to accept for my own reason is it says, "let us make man" in our own Image according to our likeness. (3:6) I see this statement as an actual statement/ proposal from one being to another of a being who was obviously present at the time of creation. (3:7) Interpret these words. To be actual words from the first mother who is God, speaking to who is the first Father which is God, about the only creation of their only children, the first daughter and the first son, who would represent woman, and man in essence. (3:8) I believe the image that the first children were created in was that they two would take on the face, body and form of an element to serve as a vessel to the existence on the physical level. (3:9) However, they also had to take on an internal form of an element to serve as a vessel to their existence on the physical level. (3:10) However they also had to take on an internal form so that they were tasked to have so that they may have the dominion over all that they were tasked to have so that they may serve as the mother and the father to all, this turning the first mother and the first father into the first grandparents. (3:11) The first daughter and the first son would take opposite e sides so that the universe so the universe may stay at a balance of peace an progress, hence the left and the right to the below and the above. The west and the east to the south and the north to the banner which is the universal compass. (3:12) All together God, God as an individual but most high god as a family. God as the universe so the introduction of the first and only children began.

(3:13) Number 3, Because again woman comes first. The first daughter, who is water? Who is dark? Who is the soul? Born in the image of the first mother so she is the gate keeper to all conscience. For it takes thought to get to creation, therefore one can only reach her mother, but through her (3:14) The first daughter, she Is the mother soul! The soul in which all souls come forth from because she was told by her parents to be fruitful and multiply. So that she did. (3:15) To multiply, she gave a piece of herself to all that live so that they may have the means to communicate with her directly, and to also have a conscience of their own to think freely for themselves. She is the universal conscience itself. (3:16) Given dominion over the brain of the body so it's where she dwells in all that live and breathe, the source of all knowledge and wisdom, she is. (3:17) Represented by the element of water, because knowledge and wisdom run as deep as a ocean. (3:18) The deeper down one soul dives, the deeper the knowledge and wisdom gets. The deeper the knowledge and wisdom gets; the closer one gets to the to the first mother who is the below itself. She is the deliverer to creation.

(3:19) One must first think first in order to create and as spoken one can reach the first mother but through her only daughter. (3.20) However created in her mother's image, she only thought, and this needed help just as her mother did. (3:21) That help came from her other half. Her brother. The Braun to her brain and was her father to her mother so he was number 4.

Chapter 4

(4:1) Because man come second to woman as light come second to dark. (4:2) The first son who is fire, who is light, who is the spirit. (4:3) Bornin the image of the first father. Tasked as the gatekeeper to all intuition, he is the father spirit in which all individual spirits come forth from. Because he was told by his parents to be fruitful and multiple, he also gave a piece of himself to all that live so that they may have a means to communicate with him directly a well as have an intuition of their own so that they may feel freely for themselves, he is the universal intuition himself. (4.4) Given dominion over the heart of the body, so it is where it dwells in all that live and breathe. (4:5) The source of all feeling and instinct. He is represented by the element of fire because feeling in instinct is the flame that burns within the earth. The stronger the intuition the bigger that internal flame gets, the higher the flame rises, the higher it rises, the higher one's spirit ascends. The higher the spirit ascends; the closer one gets to the first father who is above itself. (4.6) He is the deliverer of power. (4:7) I believe one can only reach the first father but through his only son. However, he is made in his father's image, is just the Braun. The strength and courage one need to take action whether an action be good or bad or no action at all, which is an action of its own.

(4:8) As the muscle, the spirit was created to carry the orders given by his sister the soul who is her other half, who is often misunderstood just as he is often misused.

(4:9) Created to maintain balance. The first daughter and the first son, soul and spirit conscience and intuition, the left hand, and the right, the dark and the light, the cold and the hot, dark energy light energy, the night and the day, the yin and the yang, the Bah and the Kah, most importantly, the queen and the king representing the essences of woman and man! (4:9) Women giving half of one's being as two parents must each give a child half of its chromosomes. Hence, they are together the parents that foster humanity internally. (4:10) All souls come forth from the mother soul, just as all land come from the mother land, or mother ship, mother board. If she was to cease to exist, then all consciences would sink with her causing humanity to wander about in the dark unaware of even their own existence.

(4:11) The same applies for the father spirit. For if he was to cease to exist then all intuition would seize with him causing humanity to wander about as robots, incapable of feeling any emotion for themselves, they would be heartless. (4:12) They are in all that life, tasked to take the role of mother and father to humanity, even though they didn't birth them. (4:13) They instead were born within them, so that all races and species may be connected to one set of parents, the internal parents. (4:14) Therefore were all connected to the same internal family, while physically coming from a different blood line and species.

(4:15) One may wonder or ask if a soul and a spirit are in fact the same thing. (4:16) I as a universal believe that they are both ethereal in essence. They are two sides of energy itself. (4:17) While the soul, which is the dark, which is the left, carries a negative charge or vibration that mistakenly always associated with everything good. (4:18) Almost all believe in a reality of good and evil. The darkness V.S the light, angels V.S. demons. (4.19) In all instances the dark side is always portrayed as the evil of the two, thus taught to be feared (4:20) Men of the holy bible even deemed women to be impure, as water may be before purification. (4:21) However, I believe that the condition was simply the condemnation was simply because of woman's natural association with darkness.

Chapter 5

(5:1) This is why women have either been unintentionally misunderstood, or purposely misrepresented to justify the persecution brought upon them by men of the church. (5:2) That persecution was derived from the fear that was within those men themselves a fear of the presence of dark energy itself, for the feelings of dark energy itself is that of her presence. She is the feeling of dark energy at its highest most supernatural level. (5:3) Her presence a dark mist, that brings even the courageous to fall to their faces in humanity and fear that they may be harmed by her. (5:4) for woman's association alone, a group of intentionally weak and fearful men of the past decided to change the face of history by conspiring to strip women of their place and power in humanity. This ultimately made man out to be somehow superior to women, when such was not the natural order.

(5:5) Dark energy, isn't in fact bad energy. It's just misunderstood energy based solely off of the negative vibrations, and feelings of fear and or discomfort that it produces, when it is present. (5:6) This presence is the physical presence of the first daughter and therefore predominant in woman sora, or life force.

(5:7) That consciences or subconscious fear and discomfort within those unknown men of the past is what ultimately caused almost all men to conspire against women. They promoted the idea that women uncleanness and impurity, thus demoting them to a new role in humanity and society as inferior to man.

(5:8) After eating them into submission they were given no power, or voice in the church, no power or voice in society, no power or voice in most cases even in their own homes. (5:9) Their entire existence was made to be, believed to be strictly for the purpose of tending to men. (5:10) giving them children, raising the children and keeping house while men provided all that is said to be needed. This gave man all the power, and all the say so forcing her to do all that she was told or eventually face some form of consequence, or punishment. (5:11) Any woman that didn't embrace the role as inferior to a man in society was conspired against deemed as devils, witches or whores who were then often beaten, raped, exiled, or killed. Sometimes all the above. (5:12) Women of power were beaten, violated and demeaned publicly until the surrounding and surviving women lost their will to fight ack, given to the oppression, and reluctantly embarrassed this new forced role simply to stay alive. (5:13) This role of inferiority lasted for centuries. (5:14) However, now over the last few centuries women have slowly and quietly and methodically begun to reclaim their strength and make their voices heard loud and clearly. (5:15) Year by year women grow stronger in society, and this will continue until they claim their true place in humanity as not just equal to man, but as the true leaders of men. The true navigators in which all direction truly comes from, for they have always been the mind behind all that there is. (5:16) it is now up to the strong and courageous me of the present, to right the wrongs brought upon women by the weak and fearful men of the past. Men do this gracefully and pridefully that have conditioned generations of boys that have grown to men to see themselves superior retaking their place as #2. (5:17) hence force, the muscle, the browns, the action after the order. Such is the natural order of the universe, reflected in the natural order of the mind and body itself.

(5:18) The soul gives instruction to the spirit; the spirit then gives strength from the body so that it may move to action or may not move to action. (5:19) as spoken before to not act is in fact an action of its own. (5.20) Sometimes it may take twice the amount of strength of spirit to not act in a situation depending on the circumstances. (5:21) So in that light the act of not acting is still action because it too requires strength from the spirit to carry out.

Chapter 6

(6:1) Still, the first son is intuition he can feel which instructions given are right or wrong. His natural purpose is to do whatever may be asked. However, it is up to the individual in control of their individual spirit to determine what they want to do for themselves. (6:2) They, with the gift of their own free will get to determine what kind of person they want to be. They have the strength to do their ow deeds, be they good or bad. (6:3) The first son is holy s regardless of what his strength is used for he himself will forever remain holy, in the eyes of his mother and father, who together are God. (6:4) It is an individual spirit that will ultimately be judged by the universe based off the deeds they've done in their lifetime within a particular body. All actions that will be judged. Not necessarily the actions on their own. (6:5) The first daughter is holy. Therefore, regardless of what her wisdom is used for by an individual, she will remain holy in the eyes of her mother and father who are God. (6:6) It is the individual soul that will be judged by the universe, not the mother soul herself. Still, I believe that the universe does not condemn a soul based off one having negative or positive thought alone. (6:7) instead it is intention behind the thought and the follow through, with turning the thought into an action, thus making the thought physical. That is what may be condemned by the universe because thought and intent are not always synonymous.

(6:8) The natura interaction between an individual soul and individual spirit that takes place within individuals' body, are but macrocosm of the interaction between the mother soul and the father spirit, which takes place in an unseen reality unfathomable to the average mind. (6:9) Forever my mind I believe is blessed to be above average and therefore fully capable of acknowledging that unseen reality for its insight can be endless. (6:10) Temptations of the soul are but a test. Tests, designed to aid the building of one's character. Test to establish the kind of person one will choose to be with the gift of their own free will. The soul cannot make anyone do anything, it be a good thing or a bad thing. (6:11) So believing this makes me wonder why for so long she has been blamed for all the bad or evil done in the world? (6:12) Is she to blame because she can produce dark thoughts? Thoughts of harm to oneself or other Thoughts of negativity of any form? If it's because of her ability to produce those dark thoughts, then what is that same logic not applied when it comes to the spirit. (6:13) It takes the strength of the spirit to tail a thought and turn it into action, be that action a good or bad one. Knowing this then how could the spirit always be associated with God or positive? (6:14) Spirit is ultimately the executioner of all deeds done in the world so in the light I honestly believe that he is the true beast to be feared. (6:15) Is he not the true blame for all dark deeds done? All the while still being praised for his association with the light while his sister is misunderstood and feared for her association with the dark. I believe that while spirit is indeed the savior, the Shepard and the servant. He is also a savage. The savage beast. (6:16) Truth is, that although polarity exists between the first daughter and the first son it must be understood that polarity also exists within themselves as individuals. (6:17) There is light within the dark side and darkness within the light. (6:18) This is how she can tempt with negative or positive thoughts, and he can produce negative or positive action. (6:19) Those end actions are what determine one's karmic future.

Chapter 7

(7:1) The devil in the Holy Bible, never had the power to make Jesus do anything. He just but only could tempt Jesus. (7:2) while the devil of the bible is closely associated with the soul of a person, Jesus of the bible closely associated with the spirit, so just as the soul tempts the spirit to take or not to act in my belief, I believe my understanding is metaphorically validated through the story of Jesus being tempted by the devil in the wilderness. (7:3) In the end spirit rules for Jesus relied on the strength of the holy spirit to not act when he was tempted and that action to not acted when he was tempted and that action to not act was in fact an action of itself under the universal understanding (7:4) temptation is of the mind, the mind is the soul. (7:5) Hence, the popular saying goes "Sold your sole to the devil" is but a name and image created through either a mistaken misconception, or an intended misdirection intended to misrepresent the darkness to then control the minds of the masses through their beliefs especially "African Americans" (7:6) The popular saying should instead be the opposite.

"Sold your spirit to the devil. (7:7) Because it's one's strength to act on his temptations that the devil truly wanted. Thats how one gives the devil control. By using the strength of their spirit to carry out his dark deeds. That's when one has truly sold themselves. (7:8) Whether the darkness was misunderstood or intentionally misrepresented in the past, today that distinction should be deemed irrelevant. Instead, let my understanding expose and acknowledge the unseen light of the dark so that it may be seen I the truth that it was created in. (7:9) Let this universal understanding also expose and acknowledge the unseen light if the darkness of the light so that it too may be seen in the light it was created in. (7:10) Polarity existing within polarity. (7:11) If darkness only represents bad or negative, then why is it that the first place one goes when they seek peace of mind by closing their eyelids? (7:12) They internally transport themselves to the endless abyss of darkness: Does one not go to that same abyss of darkness when they seek to meditate.... When they seek to pray to their God...... When do they seek to sleep? (7:13) Even at times one may run from the sight of something that probably scares them. To the comfort and security of internal darkness by the way of closing their eyelids. So how could the darkness be so misrepresented or misunderstood? (7:14) So while darkness is taught to be feared it's simultaneously the resting place of the mind. (7:15) remember the mind is of the soul, the soul is of the dark. Therefore, that is ultimately why I believe the dark is the subconscious refuge to ease the darkness of the minds and thoughts. For it would be back in its natural habitat. In its natural place of comfort, as a child running to their mother when afraid or unsettled in some form or fashion. (7:16) As is the same when one experiences death! For their soul returns to the mother soul so that they may rest in peace, divorced from individual thought. (7:17) The mother soul takes that burden from them and places it back in her bosom. (7:18) As the darkness of soul is misunderstood, so too is the light of spirit, in addition to being misunderstood, the spirit is also misused. (7:19) Slightly more complicated than the soul, the spirit not only has two sides, but it's also the blame for all of one's actions. (7:20) If one thinks good or bad thoughts that thought produces a feeling or vibration. That's the process of the soul ordering the spirit? The Spirit then moves the body to take or not act. (7:21) Regardless of the deed is it good or bad the spirit will oblige because its purpose of creation was to serve.

Chapter 8

(8:1) However, the spirit will instantly communicate its approval or disapproval in its language of a feeling in the heart in which drops to the stomach. Hence, the saying, "gut feeling." (8:2) there may be a heavy dark feeling, such as guilt, shame or regret, if the negative deed done or tempted to be done is approved by the spirit. (8:3) Either way whether good or bad spirit will always speak its truth.

(8:4) He will be obliged to doing a negative deed, because he knows that in the eyes of his mother and father he has done, his job and the burden of the deeds done will to ultimately be carried by the individual spirit in control of the individual body. The burden from that individual's deeds will ultimately be judged by his parents. (8:5) The father spirit himself will face no judgement or condemnation of karma, for he himself is holy. (8:6) When one hears the voice of the father spirit in the language of feeling that precedes and follows a thought or deed, The only place they can turn to, to aid their internal defense is the mother soul. She will then offer some thought of justification in one's mind in attempts to convince oneself or others that the deed done or tempted to be done had or has a just cause.

(8:7) It's like a child who does wrong, and their dad scolds them causing them to cry from the feelings that the scolding produced inside them. The child then runs to their mom to seek comfort and security. She then defends the child's actions by way of some form of advocation or justification.

(8:8) The roles of the child's parents may at times be vice versa, but the fact remains that its thought being called on to ease feeling, are the only two weapons used in the internal war of balance. (8:9) The winner of that internal war dictates action taken. The body itself is the everlasting spoils of every war that takes place within oneself! (8:10) Knowing this, one must still understand that it's the intention behind the action that lies at the center of judgment. Intention is of the heart therefore it is of the spirit and justifications that may ease an individual spirit into a false sense of delusion cannot and will never fool the father spirit himself. (8:11) He is the father of feeling; therefore, he knows any intent in one's heart before, during and after taking any action. (8:12) He is all knowing by way of feelings. He is if the first family, and the first family can't and never be fooled by one that it gave the ability to fool one too. (8:13) Praised by many as the savior, the servant and the Shepard. Spirit must be deeply analyzed to be fully understood and acknowledge to also be the snake! The savage to be feared for he is the bringer of all crisis and chaos. (8:14) Only he has the strength to murder another in any form because it takes spirit to perform those deeds from the misuse of spirit to perform bad deeds falls upon the individual spirit to be carried internally in that individual. (8:15) Feeling of regret, shame, and discomfort as well as their thoughts of guilty conscience depending upon their intention behind the deeds. (8:16) An individual's forgiveness must be earned in the eyes of the universe, then and only then may it be deemed as holy.

(8:17) The spirit, who is the father and the son, can do no wrong in the eyes of the first parents. The soul, who is the mother, and the daughter can do no wrong in the eyes of the first parents. (8:18) The two do as they were born and tasked to do. All the while, teaching molding and above all fostering the children whom they were given dominion over and responsibility for. (8:19) They both have their understanding of one another. They both understand the first mother and the first fathers' duties, and the responsibilities bestowed upon them. (8:20) Together they will uphold those duties and responsibilities without question or bias even though they understand that they don't understand humanity (8:21)

Chapter 9

(9:1) The soul and spirit balance each other. (9:2) The impure soul is purified into the holy fire as is water purified in the holy fire, as is water purified by fire. (9:3) The impure spirit is baptized in the holy water so is water able to put out the fire. (9:4) Fire cleanses the water and water Cleanses the body. (9:5) The only other way for the two to be purified or purged would be to turn to the first mother, who is earth. Instead of burning out the impurities in her daughter who is water, she can supernaturally filter them out by way of her flesh. Instead of soaking out the rage of her son, who is fire she can supernaturally entrench him with her body to keep him controlled, or she can extinguish him with her bare hand, for she is always there for her children.

(9:6) The first father who is air, may also either incite or snuff out his son who is fire, or he may harden or evaporate his daughter who is water, but himself cannot cleanse as the first mother can. (8.7) the first family is ever present. Physically Because the elements are ever surrounding. No matter where one may be at least one or more will always be there. (9:8) The first family is ever present internally because one caries them within their body and being, wherever they may go, this is how in both cases, internally and externally, the first family is all knowing, and all seeing, as God has always been spoken of to be. (9:9) I believe that God is the first parents as a union And Gods children are the first daughter and son. We are the grandchildren of God demi version of their only children. (9:10) The first the first mother is GOD, the first Father is God, the first daughter id Gods daughter. The first son is Gods son. Therefore, the earth is God, the air is God, the water is God child, The fire is Godchild. Hence forth, the south is God the, the north is God, the north is God The west is Gods child, the east is Gods child.

(9:11) The endless abyss of space one sees when they look at the stars is the infinite place of the first family. (9:12) A palace with no ceiling and no walls. A place to visit to seal in any capacity. It's where the first family does as they please, working together as a family in unfathomable ways and unfathomable places.

(9:13) They design and create planets which are, but guest houses built over time to shelter and provide for humanity making sure that humankind may have all the resources needed so they may sustain. (9:14) The first family who in plain site because they know the best place to hide the answers to creation itself was to put the answers right the face of humanity. (9:15) They know the answers would seem so simple that humanity would overlook and reject them purely based off the answer's simplicity. They would convince themselves that there had to be more to the story.

(9:16) this articulation and etheric characterization is that more to the story, humanity has seemed for so long. (9:17) The revelation of how God has always been amongst humanity, and within humanity, providing for humanity, both in this seen reality, as well as the present, yet unseen reality as well as the present, yet unseen celestial reality that exist I real time on the other side.

(9:18) Humanity continues to bleed the first family dry of their life forces, here in this guest house they've prepared so that humanity may live off the land. (9.19) the minerals of the first mother, who is earth, are greedily extracted from her womb. The cleanliness of the first father, who is air, is recklessly toxoided and polluted. (9:20) The purity of the first daughter who is water, is carelessly contaminated, tainted and desecrated, as the first son, who is fire, runs rampant, burning down it all it touches in the attempt to clear the root of the dying trees killed by loggers so that the path may be clear for the first to bring forth new life. (9:21) New life so that the ad, may once again thrive in areas injured, murdered by the grandchild which is humanity.

Chapter 10

(10:1) Humanity continues to take from the earth with no regards, as if she doesn't grow weaker with every mineral that is taken from it without being replenished. (10:2) Humanity continues to emit toxic gases into the air with no regard as if he won't one day become unbreathable to all that take his gift for granted. (10:3) Humanity acts as if the first mother and the first father will not forsake them and send their only children to purge the planet of all humankind, just as they have done before in the past. Both here as well as on other planets where humanity had done the same thing. (10:4) Yet another extension! (10:5) Blazing rocks may rain from the above and humanities abuse of the planet will ultimately render its gradually weakening atmosphere shield obsolete. Its only shield of protection from any elemental assault that may come from the above. (10:6) ferocious waters may rage and rise making oceans depths, the level of the ocean surface, while ocean's surface reaches the sky's just to fall from the clouds and wipe clean the face of the land. (10:7) The land above will become the below as nations and cities will crumble and fall to the depths of the oceans floor. Nothing or no one will be allowed to survive.

(10:8) I understand that the planet earth is a living being, has a heart in their chest, that burns with the spirit of fire, so does the planet have a heart that burs at its core. (10:9) Due to the abuse of humanity, the heart of the planet is losing its vigor, as its flame dwindles each passing century. One day its strength will no longer be able to bear the load on its shoulders.

(10:10) That dreadful day is sure a reality if more care and appreciation isn't given back to the caretaker that has already given so much., to humanity giveth, for the first family taken away.

(10:11) To be amongst God, one need opens their eyelids and seed God: open their lungs and breath God. To be amongst Gods children one needs to open their minds and understand God, open their hearts and feel god. lastly and most importantly, live a balanced life and be a vessel of God. (10:12) Be a servant Godin the family of God. because as spoken god has a family, and the family of God is everywhere. (10:13) to tune into God one needs only one tune into the universe on the 4 levels of God that are the 4 directions of God. The emotional, which is the south. The mental, which is the north. The physical, which is the west. And the spiritual which is the east. (10:14) The universe is always awaiting that human covenant and connection, but until one can connect on those 4 levels then one will never fully experience or understand what it means to be made whole. (10:15) Nor will they ever be able to understand or take their place amongst the first family which all humanity shares together.

(10:16) The first mother and the first father who are the first and second element. The first daughter and son who are the third and fourth element. Humankind is the 5th element.

(10:17) Humanity is the life representing mountain that sits at the center of the universal compass. Surrounded at all sides and angles by the life growing tree of the south, the life giving bolt of the north the life sustaining wave of the west and the lifesaving flame of the east. (7.18) The 5th element, that brings stability and security both metaphorically and physically. (10:19) The element embedded into the lifeforce of those who poses a unique internal load baring strength that often comes with more responsibility than others. (10:20) One that can only be carried by those hand chosen by the first family. (10:21) The 5th element. Rock! Crown of all creation! The element in which humanity represents so we are.

Book Of The Rock

Number 5... The 5th element,

Rock: A mineral of the earth. A Diamond, a Gemstone, a Ruby, a Crystal, Gold, Silver, {Platinum or any other solid mineral deposit, such as steel, iron, copper, tin, etc. produced in many different shapes, colors, sizes, and weights. Rock! (10:1) Its fittingly the elemental representation of humankind's place amongst the first family of creation. The 5th element, at the center of the 4 powers, the heart of the universal compass.

Chapter 11

(11:1) There are variations of the 5th element. I believe that time metaphorically exemplifies the ways in which humankind is reliable to the element itself. (11:2) First, like all diamonds and other gemstones are created in various hues of color. (11:3) Humans, Animals, and plants are created with different skin tones, different fur colors and leaf colors as well.

Just as there are many different types of rock that represent the element. I understand that there are many different types of species that represent humankind. (11:4) Just as there are many different sizes, height and weighted rock, there are different sizes height and wight people, animals and planets. (11:5) I understand that there are load baring rocks that serve as the foundation or cornerstone to smaller rocks and large structures, just as there are people, animals and plants that metaphorically serve as the foundation or corner stone to their families. (11:6) They are the support that keeps their families secure, ground and stable.

(11:7) I understand that some people who serve as the rock.

'Have larger families to support, or more people that look to them for support outside their families. Therefore, I believe God Bestowed upon them a more load barring internal strength so that they may have the ability to uphold all duties and responsibilities placed on their shoulders.

(11:8) However I believe, the most accurate similarity between the 5th element and humankind is internal. Just as precious diamonds and gemstones are supernaturally created through a process of intense pressure and intense heat applied to the rock itself. I believe people are shaped and molded on an internal level by the metaphorically intense pressure and metaphorical intense heat of their life experiences!

(11:9) The more pressure and heat applied, the larger the rock can become, enabling it to not be subjected to cracking into pieces. (11:10) I believe the same can be said in relation to people. The more metaphorical pressure and heat in one's life experience. Believe the larger the internal rock within them becomes.

(11:11) There maybe a time where the pressure may be too intense for a rock, just as there may be a time where the pressures of life for a person of life may be too intense for a person causing them both respectively to crack or even at time shattering one physically and the other internally. This may result in a rock cracking into pieces never to be fully made whole again. Just as a person could crack or shatter internally, and never be able to reconstruct well.

(11:12) Someone to support them so that they may retain the strength they need to support those who need them. Someone to help them go through things in their own lives because many will take from one life, and few will ever give back. Such is their nature. (11:13) Everyone needs someone or something!

(11:14) To one person, their rock may be their spouse or lover, to another their rock may be a grandparent, parent, sibling, relative or close friend, anyone with any standing in another's life can be someone's rock for it's a universal role, with no set face or timeline.

(11:15) The role can also be at time spontaneously situational. I also understand there could possibly be a time where a stranger can be one's rock, to help to keep their spirits high and their soles at peace. Such can be there rock (11:16) Lastly, I believe the role of the rock may be given to a thing, anything that has a connection of sentiment, such a prayer beads, religious books or any personal items belonging to loved ones, whether they are still alive or those that have since passed on to the other side of life.

Whatever it is, The rock it maybe any person. (11:17) Any person, place or thing that has the power and ability to keep one grounded when the restless waves of the mind ocean rage or the scolding flames of the hearts fire spread.

(11:18) then they are the rock and should be appreciated and referred to as such.

(11:19) Let those words and the message of my understanding become the rock, to someone, somewhere who is suffering silently in some way. Whether that way be emotional in nature, mental in nature, physical in nature, or spiritual in nature. (11:20) Just as the holy bible may be to a Christian, the Quarn may be to a Muslim, just as an oral account may be to an indigenous people such as the native to his sacred land taken and renamed America. (11:21) Let this understanding be their Rock. If they have no place else to comfortably rest their faith and understanding of a higher power.

Chapter 12

(12:1) Let that higher power be the universe, the universe as a family, the universe as the first family. (12:2) A Holy family initiated by the first family of the church, imitated by the first family of the white house, for it's the first family that imitated first families of the white house, for it's the first family that those imitated the first family was ideally derived from. (12:3) let those find their place amongst the elements of Rock, their place amongst the first family of creation. (12:4) If one so rejects then still let them know that their seat amongst the mountain of rock will forever remain open, Which I believe is sculpted to only sit them.

(12:5) Let these words put forth by the universe, through the vessel of "Rock" do as the words put forth by the chosen to teach the teachings of the teacher. Chosen to perform the depths of the doer, chosen to establish a community of a line minds that allow this message into their hearts.

(11:6) "This Rock", The light to those that travel life's roads in spiritual darkness with no comfortable place to rest their faith. (12:7) This rock star to the North that guides the way for the lost seeker. (12:8) This Rock the Alpha and the Omega…. The first and the last….

(12:9) I'AM…… North Rock…. (12:10) The Rock of salvation.

(12:11) And surely, I am coming quickly!

www.ingramcontent.com/pod-product-compliance
Lightning Source LLC
Chambersburg PA
CBHW032142040426
42449CB00005B/358